James Aquila Spurlock

A Philosophy of Heaven, Earth, and the Millennium

James Aquila Spurlock

A Philosophy of Heaven, Earth, and the Millennium

ISBN/EAN: 9783337236960

Printed in Europe, USA, Canada, Australia, Japan

Cover: Foto ©Thomas Meinert / pixelio.de

More available books at **www.hansebooks.com**

A PHILOSOPHY

OF

HEAVEN, EARTH,

AND THE

MILLENNIUM.

AND GOD CALLED THE FIRMAMENT HEAVEN.—*Gen.* 1. 8.

BY

JAMES A. SPURLOCK

A Member of the Missouri Bar.

W. J. GILBERT, PUBLISHER,
NO. 209 NORTH FOURTH STREET, ST. LOUIS, MO.

Trade Supplied by

ST. LOUIS BOOK AND NEWS CO. AMERICAN NEWS CO., of New York.
CENTRAL NEWS CO., of Phila. NEW ENGLAND NEWS CO., of Boston.

Stereotyped by STRASSBURGER & DRACH,
St. Louis, Mo.

MO. REPUBLICAN PRINT.

PREFACE.

In presenting this small book to the public, I claim that it contains a correct key to the motions of the heavenly bodies which will in the future become the basis of all true astronomy and philosophy of the movements of the heavenly bodies. My theories of heat, cold, and the seasons, will be established by the practical tests of science.

Perhaps I owe the religious world an apology for the plain manner in which I have assailed their creeds and ceremonies. These have been the subjects of so much strife, dissension, and cavil, and militate so directly against Gospel truth, that I have condemned them as heresies and idolatries. In doing so I do not question the sincerity of any church, minister or person, nor have I written in the interest of any. 1 belong to no church organization and have no partiality for any, and highly approbate the efforts of all.

As to my views of the Millennium, I have appended them to interest the reader, and at the same time silence the croakings of false prophets.

Respectfully,

JAMES A. SPURLOCK.

Versailles, Mo., January 8, 1869

CONTENTS.

CHAPTER I.
INTRODUCTION.

CHAPTER II.
THE CREATION.

CHAPTER III.
THE EARTH.

CHAPTER IV.
MAN.

CHAPTER V.
THE RESURRECTION.

CHAPTER VI.
THE MILLENNIUM.

HEAVEN, EARTH, AND THE MILLENNIUM.

CHAPTER I.

INTRODUCTION.

REMARKS—GOD—THE CREATION—THE BIBLE—AUTHOR'S POSITIONS —NATURE OF EARTH—OF THE FLESH—RESURRECTION—GRADES IN HEAVEN—WORKS STAMPED ON US—GOLDEN RULE THE TRUE RELIGION—GOD'S IMPARTIALITY—MILLENNIUM—SCIENCE.

Upon a careful survey of the heavens, all rational beings are forced to acknowledge that there is an omnipotent God who has created the heavens and the earth; but *how* and *when* are the most perplexing questions that ever presented themselves to the human mind. Where does the all-powerful Architect reside. what is the nature of His existence, and in what portion of His immense structure does he enjoy His labors and give laws to countless millions of worlds? From whence issue the

2

edicts governing the mighty hosts of heaven, and the beings who inhabit the same? What causes the pain, desire, toil, misery, strife, and death, inflicted on that part of His creation known as earth—this world which we inhabit.

Mankind in all ages have been prone to have these questions solved; but few, however wise and learned, inspired or prophetic, have attempted a solution of them. They have been content to acknowledge the existence of the vast creation surrounding them, and trace and ferret out the never-changing laws which govern the universe; but in what manner or by what means, and at what time or times, this omnipotent task was performed or accomplished, or where the mighty Creator lives, or in what portion of His domain He exerts his limitless power, has been, and is, a mystery to the mortals of the earth.

In this work I propose to give my views on these matters as succinctly as possible, and in language that will be understood by all, learned and unlearned, young and old; and in doing so, let me inform the reader that it is no part of my design to interfere with the teachings of the Bible or the doctrines of Christianity, and it is still further from my design to interfere with the doctrines of any religious denomination, but that I expect to treat the subject freely and truthfully. I maintain that religion and the Gospel are nothing more than truth, and that the teachings of any book or sect, if in accordance with truth, is Gospel and religion; and if contrary to truth, that it is of earth, and has no divinity whatever, and is not to have the sanction of our judgment.

I acknowledge the moral precepts of the Bible, and the divinity of Jesus Christ; in fact, I look to the teachings of David. Moses, and the prophets, and of Christ and his apostles, for much of the philosophy which I shall advance; and while there is no moral precept in the Bible that I am not cheerfully willing to sanction, and even be judged by, yet I must confess that there are some mere historical matters in it which are by no means intelligible to me, and which cannot be reconciled with truth and other teachings of the Book.

But these apparent inconsistencies have nothing to do with either the present or future of man. Our whole duty to God and our fellow-creatures of earth is so plainly set forth in the Bible that none, however ignorant, need err.

I shall endeavor to prove in this short work that there is an all-wise, omnipotent, and infinite creator, called God; that He is the Chief Architect and Governor of the whole universe; that He governs the same by laws just, uniform, and forever unchangeable; and, consequently, shall deny special providences or partiality in His administration. I shall endeavor to demonstrate that all His creation is good, and the enjoyments thereof all-enduring, except earth, mankind, and the creatures of earth; that desire, pain, toil, misery, and death, exist nowhere but on this earth; and that man's transgression is the cause of his own misery and death, and so of all the creatures of the earth. I deny that the creatures of earth are suffering for Adam's transgression, and shall contend that they are suffering for their own sins, of like nature with Adam's, and that the earth is the sphere in which they must repent and be regenerated through carnal death, and thus restored to heaven.

I contend that the earth is accursed of God, and not visited by Him or His angels, from the fact that all its elements are in a state of strife and war, and not suitable to be visited by holy beings; that the mortality or flesh of the earth is synonymous with the term "satan" or "devil," and the spirits of which have once enjoyed a pure and holy estate in heaven, and will again, by force of God's immutable laws, in some state, however degraded and humble, or however excellent and exalted, this to be determined by their own conduct; that we are endowed with the spirit of God, and possess most of the reasoning powers of angels, though condemned in the flesh, and to the flesh; that this spirit and reason is the gift of God, and is indestructible, and cannot, and will not, ever die, that this spirit and reason continually admonish us of our lost condition, and point us the way to heaven, our proper abode; that

they inherently have and teach the commandments of God, and plainly and imploringly
urge us to the strict performance of our duty
to God and man and the creatures of earth;
that our corporeal bodies are of earth, and are
continually prompting us to deeds of evil and
sin; that a separation between soul and body
occurs under certain defined laws of nature;
that these very laws have power to, and will,
resurrect and exalt to heaven all creatures of
earth having the spirit of God within them;
and that the spirit of man, when released
from its carnal abode, takes its flight to its
Creator, where it receives a reward suitable
to its merits or demerits on earth.

I will not teach that a small, limited space
is heaven, but will endeavor to show that it
embraces the whole boundless universe; that
the whole starry firmament above and around
us is heaven, and that it possesses the power
to give life, to destroy temporal things, and to
resurrect the souls of every creature of earth
to a pure and better existence than earth af-
fords; that this power will resurrect all crea-

tures of earth that have ever existed in the past, that now exist, or that will exist in the future; that there is no necessity for any creature of earth, however small or insignificant, to be lost for want of ability to resurrect or room to protect and accommodate it; that God in His beneficence and omnipotence has provided, and will eternally provide, for all His creatures.

I shall contend that there are grades in heaven, and that every creature of earth will in the resurrection be assigned to a place and rank in heaven suited and appropriate to its work and conduct in life; that this reward is given and place assigned immediately on the death of the creature, and that this reward depends on the performance of the duties which God has plainly dictated to all, civilized and enlightened, heathen and pagan.

I contend that our conduct on earth towards our fellow-man, God, and His creatures, will as effectually and thoroughly stamp our rank and character in heaven, as the founder's patterns stamp impressions on his wares; that this is so effectually done that there can be no deception in heaven; and that the least in heaven might judge the soul in the resurrection as accurately as a mathematician can solve a simple problem, and this without the aid and despite of prayer and rituals.

I further maintain that there are only two Gospel commands: first, supreme love to God; second, to love our neighbor as ourself. These include the Golden Rule, and should include all the spiritual teachings of the ministry. They are the substance of the Gospel and religion, while all forms of worship and ceremonies of the churches are mere shadows, and are apt too often to lead away from the performance of plain religious duties; and when they really do so, they become not only reprehensible, but degrading and damnable in their nature. Hence I condemn the doctrines of men. and teach a strict observance of the Golden Rule, from the cradle to the grave, as the only means of obtaining any excellent estate in heaven.

Our reward in heaven will depend entirely

on the performance of the various duties imposed upon us by the exigencies of this rule, and this without the aid of prayer or ceremonies. In other words, we must perform this great mandate of heaven, both to God and to man, and to the creatures of earth, and not trust to prayer and ceremonies for an acquittance from its duties.

Our Creator's laws are positive and unchangeable, and are also just and perfect, and His administration of them the most impartial; and they cannot, and will not, and should not, be relaxed on the supplication of any. They will not be suspended in their operation for any, however pious and excellent; and a person might as well endeavor to gain an exalted state in heaven by legerdemain or slight-of-hand as to gain it by the performance of rituals and ceremonies, or by prayer or confessions, without the performance of the Golden Rule and the religious duties it requires to be performed.

By our works or fruits we must be known; and our works or fruits, or deeds done in the

body while on earth, will be so indelibly
stamped upon us, or placarded on our future
existence in heaven, that God, nor His angels,
nor the least of His creatures, can be deceived
by us.

The deeds or works themselves are the means
of judgment, and are only to be observed and
noticed by the powers of heaven. As well might
a goat pretend that he was an ox, or a dog
that he was a horse, as for an extortioner to
pretend that he was a benevolent man, inclined to love and charity; or the hypocrite to
pretend that he was a sincere, well-meaning
Christian. All deceptions are impossible, for
our works will show for themselves, either to
our honor and glory, or to our degradation and
shame.

The world which we inhabit is one of strife,
sin, pain, and death, and was so designed by
the Creator. Heaven is pure, sublime, glorious, and the never-ending, all-abounding, and
eternal abode of God and all His creatures.

The whole heavens are free to the righteous
and elect of God, but the higher estates are

accessible only to few, and these few will be those who have obeyed His commandments in humility, and have not been found wanting in deeds of love and charity while sojourning on earth. Many expecting these higher estates will fall short of their enjoyment, and doubtless many an humble soul will find itself unexpectedly rewarded with them.

I propose, further, to show that the way of the Millennium, or the second advent of Christ and the angels of heaven on earth, is to be prepared by dispelling strife, pain, hunger, thirst, sin, desire, and death, from the earth, and that this will be accomplished by the appearance and passage of a heavenly body in its regular orbit, more magnificent and luminous (from its proximity to our earth) than the sun, and which will for the time so overcome the effects of the sun and the elements of earth, as to produce peace and serenity on the whole earth, during which Christ and the angels of heaven can visit the earth, and promulgate the Gospel of Truth; and that from these millennial events the Ancients derived their knowledge of the creation of the heavens and the earth, and of the fall of man.

In the meantime, I expect to advance an entirely new doctrine of the philosophy of heat, cold, and the seasons, and also of the motions of the heavenly bodies. In this I will show that light (or the sunbeams of heaven) is one of the most powerful elements of the heavens; that by its power ponderous worlds are supported and driven in their orbits. The primary planets are driven by the light of the sun around which they revolve. and the secondary planets, such as the moon, &c., are driven around the earth and other primary planets by means of reflected light and the light of the sun. I expect to show conclusively that the light of the sun causes the earth and other planets to revolve on their own axis, producing day and night; also, that heat and cold exist only on the earth, and are but properties of our own atmosphere.

As to the nature of God, it would be presumptuous for benighted man to speak of it. I shall, therefore, confine myself to results or effects, and leave the reader to form his own idea of God's existence and abode; for if we should see Him every day, our senses are too imperfect to recognize Him or the nature of His existence.

CHAPTER II.

THE CREATION.

GRANDEUR AND IMMENSITY OF HEAVEN—EMBRACES THE UNIVERSE —NATURE OF GOD—WRITINGS OF MOSES—MAN AN OUTCAST FROM HEAVEN—SIN AND DISOBEDIENCE—STRIFE OF EARTH—NATURE OF ANGELS—OF HEAVEN—GRADES IN HEAVEN—ALL TO BE RES- URRECTED—NATURE OF THE CELESTIAL BODIES—UNIFORMITY OF GOD'S LAWS—GLORY OF HEAVEN—DISCOVERY OF THE CEN- TRIFUGAL POWER THAT SUSTAINS THE HEAVENLY BODIES IN THEIR ORBITS, ETC.—THE SAME EXPLAINED—POWER OF LIGHT —REFLECTED LIGHT—DIFFERENT QUALITIES OF—A PRODUCER OF MATTER—A BEAUTIFIER—COMETS—SECOND AND THIRD HEAV- ENS—CHRIST A POWERFUL PHILOSOPHER—FINE NATURE OF THE PLANETS—OUR ATMOSPHERE THE CAUSE OF ALL OUR ILLS.

The heavens declare the glory of God, and the firmament sheweth His handiwork.

Day unto day uttereth speech, and night unto night shew- eth knowledge.—*David.*

The grandeur and sublimity of the starry heavens have in all ages attracted the attention of mankind. Even the untutored savage beholds this sublimity and grandeur, and willingly admits the existence of a Supreme Being who created them.

That heaven exists is a truth that needs no inspiration to prove, nor any prophet to teach. The fact is patent, and heaven is visible to every mortal eye, though the sight be carnal and the creature doomed to death. Heaven is spread out before and around us in one vast and eternal ocean of light, truth, architecture, and grandeur. Go and survey the same any starry night when it is not obscured by the misty clouds of the earth, or veiled by the glory of the sun, and behold a portion of its extent and sublimity! There is no mistake in the scene. The carnal eyesight is liable to be deceived, we must admit, but there is no more deception in this view than there is of our earthly existence; the one is just as patent as the other.

There are hundreds of globes and spheres, in some measure resembling this earth, that present themselves to our naked eyesight; and

when the eye is armed with the aid of powerful telescopic instruments, thousands of others
appear still farther in the distant heavens.
Many of these, without doubt, are hundreds
of times larger than our earth, and some are
smaller.   They exist of every conceivable size,
and are suited to every want, are adapted
to every enjoyment, and exist indefinitely
throughout the boundlessness of space.

Look through the vista of nature to the
ranges of enormous suns, planets and spheres,
wheeling and revolving through an immensity
of space under laws the most perfect, uniform,
and unchangeable, and ask : Who made these?
who spake them into existence? where is that
Being all-powerful enough to control the motions of that wonderful machinery? where are
the boundaries of this heavenly scene? where
are the foundations? when was this vast panorama made and spread out, and when was it
put in motion? when was the time they did
not exist? how did things appear before their
existence?

These are questions that find no solution in

the powers of earth or the mind of man; yet we must admit they have a solution, for there is certainly no effect without a cause, and these great results or effects as certainly have a cause as any other matter in existence, and that cause is God and the powers of heaven.

The omnipotent God who created the heavens and earth has, for just reasons, no doubt, concealed many of its mysteries from our view and comprehension; and as to many of the laws of nature, we are in a world of darkness. That is, man on earth is shorn of many of his faculties, among which is spiritual sight, and therefore cannot see God and the hosts of heaven; but that is no more evidence that He and His angels do not exist than that the race of men on earth does not exist—because an infant in its mother's womb cannot see and understand the nature of man and his actions on earth. The time is rapidly drawing near, and is just at hand, we may say, when we will become the children of light, through death and the resurrection, and will see and know the Author of all this vast work. We are now in the flesh and in spiritual darkness; we will then be regenerated, and the vail which now enshrouds us in spiritual darkness will be lifted, and then we can behold God and His angels in their majesty and omnipotency, together with our redeemed and regenerated friends who have preceded us on earth.

As to the nature of the God of Heaven, we know from observation that He is omnipotent, all-wise, just, impartial, all-enduring, benevolent, immutable, eternal, without beginning or end. As to His shape or form, the Bible informs us that man was created in the image of God; consequently, He must be in the human shape. The Spirit of God is omnipotent—His being or body is not. The devil exists in the flesh of earth, but God does not exist in the same manner in the spirits of heaven. The devil or satan is a creature, but God is a Creator, having visible form, functions and powers. We do not see what we term the "devil" here on earth, yet he is here. If God, however, were here, the whole mortality of earth would be cognizant of the fact and see

3

His body and form. Though that body and form is of a nature unknown to us, yet it is in power, excellence, and grandeur. His power is exerted by His spirit and by the light of heaven. His biddings must be performed by the whole universal powers of heaven. His spirit animates us all, and to that extent He is omnipresent. Moses tells us that God created man in His own image. Some, however, persist that the writings of Moses need corroboration, and in some respects they may, as his narrative of the creation and events of early history are necessarily brief and figurative. But in this respect it may be safely affirmed that he needs none, for the assertion is positive; and Moses and the ancients certainly had revelations from God and His angels, which I shall hereafter endeavor to show were given to them through former millennial events, when the gospel of truth was taught and exhibited to mankind in its purity—and that Moses' account of receiving the commandments of God is a figure of a former millennium.

Our carnal sight is subject to delusion—

spiritual sight is not. We see and know that
the vast immensity of heaven exists, and that
it could not have been made for the sole comfort and edification of the corrupt and fleeting
mortality of earth, without any chance for the
creatures of earth to obtain its enjoyments.
We know that we have no chance to enjoy
heaven while on earth, except it may be the
rays and light of the same. Could such a vast
creation have been made merely as an auxiliary of the earth? Not by any means. This
earth in bulk or size is quite insignificant
compared to many of the heavenly bodies,
such as the sun and fixed stars; and the better
opinion would seem to be, that this earth which
we inhabit is merely an auxiliary to the heavens. That is, it was designed and made as
part of the heavens, and that it is the only
part of God's creation laboring under His displeasure and curse. This is the teaching of
Moses, and this is so very reasonable that he
needs no corroboration in that assertion, for
God in His omnipotence could make a paradise as easily as a hell, and did so; but by

reason of insubordination in heaven, the earth was accursed that insubordination might be punished. Hence the strife, sin, disease, pain, hunger, thirst, misery, and death, on earth. These are the results of man's transgression, and he and all creatures of earth have been cast out from heaven to earth, to atone for their deeds ; and are to be regenerated through death, and again admitted into heaven, and rewarded according to the deeds done in the flesh while on earth, whether they be good or evil. In this assertion I am corroborated by the teachings of Jesus Christ to Nicodemus— for he says that "No man hath ascended up to heaven. but he that came down from heaven." (Jno. iii. 13.)

This strife, sin, pain, death, &c., does not and cannot exist in heaven. There all is peace, love, truth, justice, purity, glory, and life eternal. A disobedient member would instantly be cast from heaven to earth, as Michael and his angels cast out the dragon and his angels into earth, (see 12th chapter of Revelations,) or as God cast out Adam and Eve into earth, (see 3d chapter of Genesis). The sublime peace, happiness and glory of heaven must, in the nature of things, be unbroken and eternal. Strife, sin, pain, nor death, cannot enter there; neither can contention, hatred, or discord, but the Christian virtues only.

The angels of heaven are doubtless endowed with great freedom of action and will, as also of power and ability. God and His angels are not mere ideal beings or nonentities, but are possessed of omnipotent and herculean powers. This reason would teach aside from revelation. Heaven is also full of grades and ranks as earth. This is according to God's justice and impartiality, and is taught by the Bible.

In speaking of the resurrection, St. Paul (1st Cor. xv. 41, 42) says, "There is one glory of the sun, and another glory of the moon, and another glory of the stars; for one star differeth from another star in glory. So also is the resurrection of the dead." Christ says, (see 14th chapter St. John's Gospel,) "In my Father's house are many mansions." St.

John in Revelations speaks of angels, and also of mighty angels; St. Paul also speaks of a third heaven, and Christ speaks of a paradise. And from divers other passages of Scripture we are bound to infer that heaven, though abounding in peace, love, glory, and eternal felicity, has grades and degrees of rank and enjoyment. The enjoyments of certain portions must be more delightful than others, and the powers and rank of certain angels much more desirable than others.

We must admit also from the teachings of Christ that there is a "strait gate," or elect portion of heaven, to which he invites us to enter, and through which none but the righteous can enter, compared to which we must reckon all else as loss. Here Christ and his exemplary followers will reign in great glory and bliss, enjoying the choicest blessings of God; but it by no means follows that this strait gate embraces the whole heavens, but only the chief or elect portion, while there are other grades passing down from this high grade to the moral people of earth—then to

idolaters—then to usurers—then to extortioners—then to oppressors of the poor—then to
liars and fornicators—then to hypocrites—
then to rogues, murderers, and beasts. All of
these latter must of necessity be debarred
from the elect and chosen part of heaven
occupied by Christ and his true followers;
hence he represents them as existing outside
of the strait gate and as suffering loss.

As to the nature of the power of angels, it is
beyond the comprehension of men to understand or explain. But we know that there
are powers which are imponderous and invisible, such as heat, cold, light, life, &c. Heat
and cold possess enormous power, so does the
light of heaven. These powers are invisible,
as philosophers say, while their effects are
visible. And so it is with spiritual power: it
is invisible, yet its effects are plainly visible.
All animal life is the result of spiritual power,
or, in other words, the life that exists in man
and animals, giving their bodies vitality, is
the gift of God, exerted by His Spirit. This
Spirit has immense force, and when withdrawn

from the subject, leaves it truly a dead, corrupt, and wrecked mass of ruin. It is this unseen power that gives life to all earthly objects subject to life and death.

Of the nature of this power we can only conjecture; philophers witness its effects, but are dumb when an explanation is demanded. It is one of the sealed mysteries of heaven, and proves conclusively that man is in a fallen state and is shorn of his proper attributes.

How unthankful mankind are to dispute or even doubt the existence of their heavenly Creator, and the resurrection and redemption through death into His eternal heavens, simply because He has not unfolded to them all the mysteries of godliness, or given them sense to comprehend the same! This light is denied for the most wise purposes. This life is at present one of trouble, anxiety, hope, and restlessness. Show men the grandeur of God and His angels, and the pure and heavenly bliss they enjoy, and are to enjoy through all eternity—make the resurrection to these enjoyments a patent and discernible fact to their sight and understanding, and life on earth itself would become intolerable and insupportable. There is enough now exhibited to satisfy all reasonable beings of these facts—the beasts of the earth recognize them.

Now, I might ask the reader to survey the starry heavens, and request him to answer where he would locate the true heaven that he has fancied as the chief resting-place and abode of the saints. If we locate it above, our antipodes, the Chinese, will probably say we have located it below. If we locate it east or west, what assurances have we that we are correct? The truth is, the heaven which we all desire to reach and enjoy, fills and embraces the whole immensity of space and eternity. That this space and heaven are without bounds or limits, either as to architecture, like the heavenly bodies, or planets, suns and spheres; or as to time, the beginning and end of which is inconceivable to the human mind.

This space is indefinite; but if the human mind, or the spirit of man, which is the true man, was once released from the flesh, or our carnal bodies, it could traverse much of this space with the rapidity of thought or light—could visit different portions of heaven, or various planets, just as quick as thought or light. Space and distance, though alarmingly great to us mortals of earth, have but little application in heaven to those who enjoy perfect gifts and entire freedom.   Doubtless many of us will be denied these gifts and freedom, and our enjoyments and capacities limited, by reason of our disobedience on earth.   Our reward must and should be according to our works.

Time has not the same meaning in heaven that it has on earth, and distance is but a small matter.   To illustrate:—Upon the death of an individual, he, or his spiritual being, is at once in the immediate presence of God and the powers of heaven, and this by instantaneous flight to heaven.   God's throne is not on earth, because it is unfit for the same; it is nothing more than His footstool.   His throne is in heaven because it is pure, holy, and sublime; while earth is corrupt and degraded.

God's abode is far removed from earth. A simple visit to our earth would be the cause of removing all strife, pain, sin, desire, and death, for the time being; and the glories of heaven, and of departed friends, would be visible to all His creatures But it is ordained otherwise, and this world must grope in darkness, sin, misery, and death, till the millennial reign, when the world will at last have a season of peace, and the true Gospel will again be preached.

That heaven embraces all space and mechanism as exhibited in the starry firmanent there is but little doubt; such was the teaching of David in the 19th Psalm. Christ spoke of "his Father's house," and represented it as containing "many mansions": this evidently had reference to the universality of heaven. This view is nowhere controverted by the Bible, and is well sustained by reason and philosophy. St. John in Revelation speaks of the New Jerusalem as coming down from God: he gives the dimensions of it. But this has no reference to heaven itself, but proba-

bly of an elect portion of it (of which I have
heretofore spoken), claimed and set apart for
Christ and his true followers. The Bible says
expressly that it came down from God out of
heaven.   This again corroborates my statement that heaven is embraced in the countless universes which eternally exist in the
boundlessness of space. It also rather corroborates my views of different rewards in the
heavens, and that every being will be judged
according to his works, and assigned to apart-
ments suited to his tastes, inclinations, and
merits.

In the first chapter of Genesis, Moses gives
an account of the creation of the heavens and
the earth. I shall now proceed, briefly, to notice his narration of the creation, lest critics
should say that I have contradicted the authority and teachings of Moses. This I have
no intention of doing, by any fair construction.
But here let me premise that we must not conclude that Moses was endeavoring to enlighten
the world with a scientific treatise on geology,
astronomy, or philosophy; neither is such

particularly my intention at present; but he was endeavoring to impress the great truth on the minds of the people that heaven existed, and that it was made by an all-wise and powerful God sufficiently omnipotent to create them according to His will and pleasure; that the same was governed by Him according to just and invariable laws. He also taught that our earth was under the curse of God for man's transgression.

At what time the "beginning" was, Moses does not pretend to say. He says, "In the beginning God created the heavens and the earth." Moses could not truthfully have stated the time of the creation only as he did; so he contented himself with the expression "in the beginning"; for time, as we use it, was not applicable to his subject. The time, in all probability, was remote, perhaps beyond human comprehension, or even calculation. Here allow me to observe that all the changes and strife of the earth are due chiefly to our atmosphere, or its action on the other elements of earth, and that the earth possesses no

elements sufficient to effect its destruction—
hence, if you will still our atmosphere, no
changes will occur on earth of any note—and
that the earth has endured and will endure
forever. I will speak more fully of the elements of earth in the next chapter.

Some persons believe that the heavens and
the earth have existed only about six thousand
years, and conclude so from the generations
recorded by Moses and the Bible. But this
world or earth may have existed, and without
doubt did exist, thousands and perhaps millions of years before Adam was driven out of
the garden of Eden into earth, and will without doubt exist as long as time endures. It is
a part of God's majestic work. It is set in motion and governed by His laws. It has no elements within it sufficient to accomplish its
own destruction. It exists according to God's
will, and unless He should destroy it Himself,
it will endure forever. This, a benevolent God
will never do. If there is any alteration in the
affairs of earth, the creatures of earth may
confidently expect to be benefitted and not

damaged by the change. He created the heavens and the earth, and from the language of Moses we must infer that they were created at the same time.

The earth was placed in its proper sphere in the solar system, and performs a journey around the sun once a year, giving us the four seasons; and revolves on its axis once in twenty-four hours, giving us day and night. It moves in its orbit and revolves on its axis with a steadiness and regularity which none but God could dispense, and which can only be interfered with by Him. So also of the other heavenly bodies; they perform their journeys and revolutions according to the will and power of God. They have no will of their own, and there is no other power higher than God for them to obey, and consequently they must obey His will. That will is unchangeable, and is the element of eternity, and will endure forever.

The vast celestial system we behold of a starry night partly composes the heavens, and is the abode of the true and living God and His angels. His existence and theirs is without beginning and without end. He has existed indefinitely and will so exist; so have and will His works, the heavens, there being no other power to destroy them.

It is evident that the earth has undergone changes by violence, and this was inflicted probably at the time it was cursed for man's trangression. However that may be, it is now the scene of continual strife, violence, change, and death. The whole powers of heaven seem to entail a perpetual warfare upon it, producing this strife, sin, decay, turmoil, change, and death. I shall speak of this more fully hereafter, and shall endeavor to trace a few of these changes and convulsions of earth to their proper sources.

But to return to the consideration of the starry heavens. I contend that each and every star placed in the heavens is the abode of angelic beings; that each one of them is but one of the mansions of the Father's house spoken of by Christ; that they have different and diversified glories as spoken of by St. Paul, and that they will afford ample room for the appropriate enjoyment of each and every creature of earth possessing the Spirit of God, though these enjoyments will be as diverse as the traits, inclinations and conduct of all that have dwelt upon the earth. In heaven's wide extent there is room for all. The most insignificant, even as the ant, need not be lost. There will be no use in sending the foolish idolaters or wicked sinners to a hell of literal fire. Their punishment before the throne of God will be just, ample, and eternal. Their shame and ignominy will be complete and humiliating. Hypocrites will no longer be stumbling-blocks, and false teachers will no longer be deceivers. Every creature's status, grade, and enjoyment, will be fixed and awarded as their works shall be. Nature teaches these lessons of degrees and ranks through all her works. The heavenly bodies teach them, the Scriptures teach them, reason teaches them, and they must be admitted as established truths.

The grades and ranks of earth will all find

4

positions in heaven. The pursuits, inclinations and enjoyments of earth will also diversify the heavens, and render them interesting and pleasing. Every imaginable grade of beings that exist on earth possessing the Spirit of God will likewise exist in heaven. The earth itself is in truth only a miniature portrait or reflex of heaven. But with all this admixture of souls and variety of beings, there will be the utmost peace, harmony, universal love, good-will, friendship, and charity. The evil dispositions of earth will be slain by death; and the creatures of heaven acknowledge God's justice and wisdom, and be content with their state and enjoyment, however degraded or meagre it may be.

All power of harm and every incentive to do wrong will be shorn from the creatures of earth by death, and they will all forever thereafter enjoy life eternal. This life eternal, however, must be subject to the holy laws of heaven; and as there is no temptation or incentive to do wrong or commit sin, if the creatures of heaven through positive and uncalled-for disobedience violate those laws, punishment, repentance, and regeneration on earth, are the consequences. This position will be more fully illustrated hereafter in the fall of Adam and Eve.

The angels of heaven undoubtedly possess free will only so far as restrained by certain positive and known laws, which extend only to preserve and protect the peace, happiness and glory of the heavens. This will—or liberty, if you choose,—is not alike to all, but is more abundant with some and contracted as to others, to be determined as their works shall be.

We behold the uniformity and certainty of God's laws in the administration of the heavenly bodies. The solar and planetary systems of the heavens are governed with accurate harmony and perfection far excelling any contrivance of man, and are suggestive of the omnipotence and wisdom of God. Observation teaches us that the laws by which God governs the universe are true, perfect, harmonious, and impartial. Not a jar, not a quiver, can be observed in the movements of the heavenly bodies. It is true there are slight variations in their courses in their orbits, but these are natural and result from attraction and repulsion, which characterizes their existence and motions. God's vast systems of heavenly architecture revolve and move in the firmament of heaven with unerring certainty and most sublime and placid harmony.

Philosophers have advanced various theories and opinions respecting the movements of the heavenly bodies, all of which have proved to be unsatisfactory. The philosophy of Sir Isaac Newton is most generally accepted. He discovered the principle of gravitation, and was also aware that there was an equally opposing force called the "centrifugal" power, but was wholly ignorant of its nature. He was misled by the teachings of his day, and, strangely enough, failed to discover it.

I claim the honor of this discovery, and will proceed to give a synopsis of this power and its effects. Newton taught that there was a "centrifugal power," which caused corporeal matter, as the earth and planets, to fly away from the sun; and that there was also an equally opposing "centripetal power," which would cause them to fly to the sun. This is the attractive power that matter has, and causes this earth and other planets and spheres to cohere or stick together. One planet possesses affinity for another, and the whole would fly together if there was not some opposing power to prevent it. The sun is much larger than all the planets revolving around it, that properly belong to our solar system. It being about fourteen hundred thousand times as large as our earth, the earth and all other planets near it would be instantly attracted to it and buried in its light (not fire, for the sun is not even hot), if they were not repulsed by the opposing centrifugal power. This is the philosophy of Newton. He was correct so far as he went, but made erroneous suppositions, because he was unacquainted with the centrifugal power which drove or repelled the planets and the earth from the sun. This power is simply the light emanating from the sun and other luminous bodies. It has not heretofore been recognized and taught as an element, and Newton was deceived thereby. Light is a powerful element, and issues from the sun and other luminaries in great volume, in every direction, and with power and velocity sufficient to repulse, drive away, or float off, the earth and other planets belonging to our solar system, to certain distances or points in the firmament which are determined in all instances according to their respective densities or affinity the sun possesses for them, and also by the power of the particular strata or rays of light in which they are placed. When thus driven away by the power of the sun's light, they find an equilibrium in it, adjusted between the centrifugal power of light, which has floated or driven them off from the sun, and the centripetal power of the sun, which attracts and draws them to it. Now, when thus floated away from the sun, they would remain stationary in the heavens, without performing any revolutions either annual or diurnal, if the sun and its light were still. But the sun is not still, neither is its light ; but the sun revolves on its own axis once in twenty-five days and ten hours, and as it revolves its rays of light also revolve with great velocity and power. These rays of light strike the earth with great projectile power on that one-fourth part next to the sun and in the rear of its course in its orbit, and projects or drives it forward in its orbit. It must go around the sun, because the particular strata of light suited to its density revolves around it, and as it revolves the earth is driven around with it. It is forced in that particular strata of revolving light, because none other suits its density. And so of all the planets. Light travels much faster than the planets and our cumbrous earth. The sun revolves nearly fifteen times while our earth makes one journey around it; consequently, revolving light travels some fifteen times as fast as the earth, and does not therefore strike the earth with any projectile force in the front of its course in its orbit, but with great projectile force in the rear fourth part next to the

sun, and thereby compels it to turn inward to
the sun, and revolve on its own axis, thus giving us day and night.

The sun revolves on its axis from right to
left, but the earth revolves on its axis from left
to right.   All the planets, as well as the earth,
are driven by the revolving light of the sun in
the same course it turns; that is, from right to
left, or from west to east.   If we were situated
below the sun's true equator, matters would
appear reversed.

Light emanates or is thrown off from the
sun and other luminaries with greater force
and velocity at its equator than at its poles.
If the planets Jupiter and Saturn were placed
over the northern and southern poles of the
sun, they would approach it much nearer, and
would not revolve in any orbit, or on their own
axis.   Light has probably the same brilliancy
in all directions from the sun and other luminaries, but not the same centrifugal or repulsive
power; hence, a comet or other celestial body
may approach much nearer to the poles of the
sun than it could to its equator.   The velocity

and power of light recedes from the sun's equator to its poles. All the planets have one hundred and eighty degrees, or one-half of them, illuminated by the sun's rays, and the other side is shaded or dark, and they all revolve on their axis, giving day and night; some, however, revolve quite slowly. This is determined chiefly by their densities and circumferences, and their poles have much influence over their diurnal revolutions. The diurnal revolutions of some of the secondary planets or satellites—our moon, for instance—are nearly destroyed by the attractions of the earth and their primary planets and by reflected light.

While the light of the sun floats off the primary and secondary planets from the sun and causes them to revolve around it and on their own axis, reflected light, combined with the light of the sun and the attractions of the sun and primary planets, causes the satellites or moons to revolve around the primary planets. Our moon, for illustration, revolves around the earth by means of reflected light chiefly, but is aided, of course, by the light of the sun and the attractions of sun and earth. At the new moon phase the moon is nearly between the earth and the sun; if precisely so, an eclipse of the sun occurs. This is but rarely so, however (and I am not speaking of such now). When thus between us and the sun, she is in the dense light of the sun and in the reflected light of the earth. This reflected light, though not powerful like that of the sun, is yet quite powerful. It has forced the moon in a strata of the sun's light which is too powerful for her density, and she is compelled to rise out apparently above our horizon in a curved line or orbit to the first quarter or half moon phase. The earth is attracting her, and the impetus the light of the sun and the reflected light of the earth has given her projects her beyond the earth's orbit, where she presents the full moon. At the full moon phase she would instantly fly to our earth, for the earth and the sun both strongly attract her in the same direction, and besides the light in that position is too rare for her density; but her own reflected light, which now strikes the earth strongly, bears her around; consequently, when she begins to approach the sun in search of a stronger light, she is borne around our earth to her third quarter: there she encounters the reflected light of the earth, and is driven on in her orbit to the new moon phase again. and thus around our earth forever. While within the earth's orbit, or between us and the sun, she is forced away by the earth's reflected light, and while without her orbit by her own reflected light. The moon is nearly of the same density of the earth, and so must all other celestial bodies be in order to approach near it.

Reflected light has and will forever prevent collisions among the heavenly bodies; for the reader must remember. that, in order to approach near each other, they must be of nearly the same density, and that a small power or force would throw or bear them around each other. If a comet should approach from within the earth's orbit, the reflected light of the earth would force it apparently above into our horizon; if it should approach the earth from without its orbit, its own reflected light would bear it around the earth.

Our solar system is an inferior one. There is another higher order of systems, and these two orders are crowned with still a third grand system. That is, there are three grades composing the heavens, and the higher grades drive comets through our solar system. These comets have immense orbits, which is proven by the fact that some of them are known to require more than five hundred of our years to complete one revolution, and perhaps some require five thousand years; for, strange as it may seem, the **heavens** cannot be spanned. No comet can complete its circle; and if one should travel in a direct line, with the rapidity of lightning, through the illimitable regions of space and through the ages of eternity, it still would not find the boundaries of heaven. God's architecture, as displayed to us partly in the heavens, is universal and eternal. These second and third systems of the heavens are perhaps of a different order to our solar sys-

tem. They are, perhaps, composed of substances and emit lights of wholly different
nature, and our sun and planets possess but
little attraction for or influence over them. In
fact, comets seem nearly independent of our
system, and must be of quite a different composition, though tangible and powerful as our
planets.

Light is a powerful element which gently
and thoroughly fills all space, and imperceptibly exerts great power. Its regularity and
mildness are suggestive of the purity, eternity
and serenity of heaven, and the impartiality
of God. By its power, all the creatures of
heaven and earth are more or less affected.
Even the creeping vine, if growing in the
shade, is attracted to its presence. Corn, and
other vegetation, if planted in the shade, are
drawn to it if there is a crack or opening near
enough to admit its rays. Vegetation naturally seeks the light as if by instinct. It is
the power of light that causes vegetation to
spring upward. The light invites and attracts
it upward, as if to bid it to a higher and better

element. If light did not possess this power and attraction, seeds when germinating would be as likely to cast their shoots downward, or laterally in the earth, as to burst forth into the light above. So with the souls of earth. On the new birth, or resurrection of the dead, we are compelled by the attraction of light to appear before the throne of God, which is vivid with intense light; but not so with heat. This resplendent light is the ordeal that tries men's souls, and shows up all their deeds to the gaze of heaven, whether they be good or evil.

Light is the agent by which God governs the universe. It drives the planets in their orbits, and causes them to revolve on their axes, giving day and night. It also gave them their rotundity. If it were possible to extinguish the light of the sun, all the planets belonging to our solar system would instantly be attracted to it. It is also the chief agent by means of which God created the universe. The heavens, according to Christ, grew as from a grain of mustard-seed, and are in all probability yet growing and increasing. He also taught that they not only grew, but that they were spread out as if by leaven; and by this word "leaven" he simply meant light. Here we find a God-like man asserting, upwards of eighteen hundred years ago, that the heavens grew, and were spread out by light or leaven; which is the most rational philosophy of the heavens that has ever been advanced. His assertion was truth and not theory. He possessed the power of seeing men's souls and observing their thoughts, just as we see men's bodies and observe their motions. He saw the heavens and the creatures thereof in their spiritual and true light, a view which is unknown to us. This view enabled him to heal the sick, feed the hungry, and raise the dead. The causes of desire, life, and death, were clearly seen and understood by him. By this view, he resisted the temptations of Satan; for he saw God and the angels of heaven beholding his trial, and the majesty and splendor of God's kingdom and the bliss of His people or angels made Satan's offer to appear as dross. For this reason Christ was indifferent to the

wealth or honors of this world, and of the applause of men.   As soon as his mission was
performed, he saw the glory displayed to
which he was to return ; hence he went to his
own funeral as cheerfully as a bridegroom to
his marriage.

Light emanates from the sun's equator in a
direct line, at right angles with its poles.   As
it issues from the sun above or below its equator, it forms a less angle with its poles, till it
reaches them.   A planet situated in its equatorial light, a billion of miles from it, would
revolve in an immense orbit; while, if situated
the same distance from it, but in light emanating from near its poles, it would revolve in
quite a small orbit. Those planets revolving in
the largest orbits are, perhaps, situated in a
stratum of light issuing from the sun's equator,
because light is thrown off stronger there than
elsewhere.   Two bodies of different densities
cannot approach each other very closely, as
they cannot remain in the same stratum of
light. Bodies of small densities may apparently attract each other in their orbits, in a rare

light, as much as bodies of greater densities in a denser light.

Our philosophers inform us that there are but few planets belonging to our solar system. Eight planets, besides the asteroids, include all belonging to our system, to-wit, Mercury, Venus, the Earth, Mars, Jupiter, Saturn, Uranus, and Neptune. There are a number of satellites or moons, and it is now said that there are about one hundred of the asteroids, but few of which, if any, are visible to the naked eye. It is also said that the planes of all their orbits are, and must of necessity be, through the centre of the sun. That is to say, if a carriage-wheel correctly represents the solar system, the hub would represent the sun, and all the planets must revolve around it at various distances, but between it and the rim or tire; or, if beyond that, they must be in a direct line, as the spokes point. Now, it is more than probable that all the planets do not thus revolve, with the planes of their orbits through the centre of the sun, but may, and in fact do, revolve in a light far above or below

6

the sun's true equator, with the planes of their orbits far above or below its centre. They may revolve in a light issuing from the sun's northern or southern hemisphere; and it is questionable if there are not numerous planets belonging to our system which have been classed as fixed stars. If, however, philosophers can establish the fact, that all the planets have the planes of their orbits through the centre of the sun, then they establish the fact that the matter composing this earth and all the other planets has been thrown off from the sun at its equator only, owing to the greater centrifugal force produced thus by its revolution on its own axis.

Every planet is driven or floated off to its proper position in the firmament by the power of light. They are the products of light; they are indebted to it for their revolutions around the sun and on their own axes; they are also indebted to it for their rotundity and for their oblate or spheroidal form; and our earth is indebted to it for its inclination on its axis, (which is probably a depression and elevation below and above the sun's equator), giving us the seasons.

Our philosophers suppose that this earth and the other planets may have been violently stricken off from the sun, or that they were made and with great power cast off, at right angles with the sun, into open space, by an all-powerful God, and that between a momentary impulse thus given and the great attraction the sun possesses for them they have found their present orbits. God never performed His work in such a fortuitous manner. He created and arranged the heavenly bodies in such systematic order that durability, harmony, grandeur, and eternity, are the results. System and order reign, and the heavens increase eternally.

Many will disagree to the proposition that the earth is growing in size, but geology and critical examination and reason prove such to be the fact. The different strata of our earth also demonstrate it. The primary stratum was made long before the curse of God was pronounced on the earth, because no traces of vegetation, man, or the animals, are to be found in it. No evidences of change, misery, or death, are to be found. This primary stratum lies deep in the earth, unless it has been disturbed by volcanic action. Next we find the secondary stratum or formation. This is above the other, and in it we find the evidence of change, suffering, and death, as regards vegetation and the animals, for their remains are clearly seen it. And finally in the tertiary or third formation, near the surface, we find the remains of man. This coincides with the Mosaic account, and clearly proves that the earth increases in size. It also proves that the angelic beings who inhabited this earth prior to its curse, which was simply clothing it with the atmosphere, were not subject to death. It cannot be doubted that the earth, and all the planets, fixed stars, and suns, are and always were inhabited. Nature teaches that the whole creation is teeming with life, and Christ taught that there was life, and life more abundant, and life everlasting, in the heavens.

The different formations above alluded to, all characterized by different phenomena and marks, and all denoting different eras, prove conclusively that the earth grows in size, and consequently that Christ's assertion that the heavens grew, is a truth. The soil on which we now walk and have our existence will, in the distant future, be buried miles beneath the surface. "Every valley shall be filled, and every mountain and hill shall be brought low; and the crooked shall be made straight, and the rough ways shall be made smooth." (See 3d chapter of St. Luke.) This, however, will require thousands of centuries and perhaps millions of years to complete it, but time will accomplish it. This growth is so gradual and imperceptible that neither animal nor vegetable life is or will be affected by it. It will also be accomplished in such a manner that the water and dry land will keep pace with each other; not that light first produces water, but that it produces earth, minerals, and water, at the same time, which are separated by means of the atmosphere; and when thus separated, each seeks its place under the laws of attraction and gravitation. If this hypothesis is correct, the sea rests on the primary formation, and does not extend very far into it. Water does not penetrate or extend into the earth very deep, for the reason that there was no atmosphere by whose action it was separated from earthy and mineral substances. Hence, if the theory is correct, the earth is all a solid a short distance below its surface.

Can it be possible that all space between the planets is devoid of matter. Philosophers so teach, and further suppose that if a planet was once set in motion in this void space by a projectile force, that its motion would continue forever despite the attraction of the sun. This cannot be admitted as truth. The perpetual attraction of the sun would soon arrest the single impulsive movement of a planet even if space was void of matter, because a continuing force or power produces more effect than an impulsive or projectile one. Besides, there are not any portions of the heavens or interplanetary space that are devoid of matter, as light is matter, and withal a most powerful element.

Why is it that the planet Mercury, having a density double that of this earth and situated twice as close to the sun as this earth, moves in its orbit only a little faster than this earth? If Mercury maintains her position in her orbit by a projectile force given her in the beginning, that force must have been immense, and her velocity astonishingly great, in order to resist the constant attraction of the sun. But her motion in her orbit around the sun is, comparatively speaking, only a little faster than our earth. This proves that the planets are not driven in their orbits around the sun by a simple, instantaneous, projectile force, but by a power that is constant, uniform, equable, and eternal; and this power is the light of luminous bodies.

The reader must remember that the motion of the planets around the sun is not denied. Latitude and longitude are correctly ascertained by the motions of the planets, and by observation of the fixed stars. But it is contended that light is the chief cause of every motion or movement among the heavenly bodies. There is a centripetal power which causes matter to approach matter, and to adhere or stick together. This power Newton discoverd and explained. There is also a centrifugal power, which causes matter to fly off from matter, as the planets fly off from our sun. No philosopher has ever explained the nature of this power. Light, I assert, is the centrifugal power of the heavens; and in so saying, no man's philosophy is contradicted, but a vacuum is supplied. Nature and the motions of the planets prove my assertion to be true.

I wish the reader further to remember that I do not claim that my theory is perfect in every particular, or that my assertions are infallible. I do claim, however, that the general principles stated are correct, and that details can, and will be, accurately made in the future.

There is not the least possible chance for a collision to occur among the heavenly bodies. Take this earth, if possible, hundreds of millions of miles farther from the sun, and when released it will sink back to its orbit. In its flight and haste to reach its orbit, it would pass it and approach very near to the sun, and then vibrate a few times within and without its orbit, but it would quickly find its proper orbit, and revolve as now. Take it, if possible, to the sun, and the light of the sun would repulse it back to its orbit, because there is found its only proper equilibrium and place. Remove all the planets much farther from the sun, and they will sink back to their orbits. Bring them, if possible, into a small group around the sun, and its light will drive or float them to their present respective orbits, for there are no other strata of light suited to them. For this reason, if the whole created heavens were gathered into a grand constellation, the power of their luminaries, exerted through their light, would spread them out again.

Light is a powerful element, and possesses great repulsive or floating power. This may appear incredulous to many, but everything is after its own kind, as nature teaches as well as the Bible. Everything is adapted to its own element: dirt and slime for worms, water for fishes, air for man and animals, and light for the heavenly bodies, God, and the angels. The frog would not exchange the slime of his pond for the elegance of the king's palace. Let the reader observe the worms of the dirt and the fishes of the sea. If they are conscious that they are in an element, they have not any knowledge that air is an element; yet air is an element much more important than water. If you deprive the worm or fish of its element it must die, and so with man; not because there are no other elements, but because there are no others suited to the organization of their corporeal existence. A whale or porpoise would consider our atmosphere an ideal thing, possessing no reality, and just so have mankind considered light. Light is a glorious element, the highest known to nature, and is the supporter of the starry heavens. Let me ask the doubting philosopher, why he has written and discoursed so much on a mere non-entity, if light is such. Why has he delivered so many lectures on a thing that has no existence? Why has the medical man lectured and cautioned the world concerning the beneficial effects of light on the constitution and health? Why is it so necessary to the husbandman, in order to make and secure good crops? Why will philosophers and astronomers proclaim that the sun, moon and stars hang upon "nothing," when the heavens are teemingly illuminated with light so powerful as to support and float these celestial bodies in their proper orbits and places? Why proclaim to benighted man, that if our earth, or any other planet, should lose its equilibrium for a moment, it would be attracted to the sun, or fly off into a void or unknown space, probably making a wreck of itself and other planets, if not the whole heavens? These are questions that cannot be answered except by adopting my philosophy.

Light has a powerful effect on the earth and the creatures of the earth. When we are in good health, its effects are natural and imperceptible, just as water is to the fishes; but if

our health is bad, and the system quite feeble,
then its effects become visible. The fishes feel
no inconvenience from the pressure of water,
neither does man nor the beasts from the ordinary pressure of light and air. The corporeal conditions of each are adapted to its own
elements.

Light also begets or produces matter, as the
earth, planets, &c.; and as there are different
kinds of light, they, each one, produce and
bring forth matter after its own kind, just as
the visible objects of earth produce and bring
them forth.

Christ was a powerful philosopher, and fore-
shadowed the philosophy I have advanced,
and is really entitled to the honor of it; and if
philosophers will honestly consult his teachings, especially his similitudes of the kingdom
of God (see 13th chapter of St. Luke's Gospel),
I doubt not they will agree with me in saying
that those very similitudes prove his divinity,
and consequently his positive teaching of the
resurrection of the dead. He said of the kingdom of God, " It is like leaven which a woman

took and hid in three measures of meal, till
the whole was leavened." The word "leaven"
there used means light; the "three measures
of meal" represent the three different grades
of heaven, as the first, second, and third heavens; the word "hid" signifies undiscovered or
unobserved, as it was at that day. St. Paul
also spoke of "the third heavens," and he sol-
emnly affirmed that he obtained his knowledge of Gospel truths from heaven, and not
from men.

Christ, in his first similitude, likens the
kingdom of God to "a grain of mustard-seed,
which a man took and cast into his garden,
and it grew and waxed a great tree, and the
fowls of the air lodged in the branches of it."
Now, from this similitude we may very properly infer that the heavens have been produced
by a natural growth, and not made with God's
own hands, and cast out in void space, as some
philosophers have imagined. The planets are
the products of light. Light represents "the
garden," the sun represents the "grain of mustard-seed," "the fowls of the air" represent the

angels of God. The heavens have thus been
grown and produced by the power of light, under the all-wise and omnipotent superintend-
ence of God and His mighty angels.

If Christ had given the world a true and
plain explanation of the philosophy of heav-
en, or even that of earth, in his day, he would
have been accounted a maniac and impostor,
and his teachings of holy truth ignored by the
world. He knew this, and said milk was fit
for little children. He also rebuked his apostles because they applied his teachings to
worldly things. His apostles were continually
misunderstanding him also; but he knew
abundantly well that succeeding generations
would acknowledge his divinity, and that science would corroborate his teachings. He was
talking of " light" and the "children of light"
after he made these similitudes, and so were
his apostles; and there was a very powerful
meaning attached to such remarks; and if our
learned divines would endeavor to ferret out
such, instead of disputing over senseless
creeds and meaningless ceremonies, they

would promote truth and Christianity much more.

Paul, in the first chapter of his epistle to the Romans, says, "For the invisible things of Him from the creation of the world are clearly seen, being understood by the things that are made, even His eternal power and Godhead." So we may infer that God and His infinite power can be understood by man, and that science will develop matters of the most astounding nature, and that before many centuries, or years, even.

Some kinds of light beget or produce comets. These bodies must be composed of matter quite different from our earth, and in all probability of much finer material or texture; and perhaps there are other bodies still finer. Some philosophers affirm, or conjecture at least, that these comets are merely nebulous matter, or will-o'-the-wisps. If such be the fact, then so are all the planets and the heavenly bodies, and the earth is one vast grave-yard, and there is no resurrection or place for any beyond the tomb. Such is, to say the least of it, sheer nonsense. Comets are corporeal, tangible bodies, of excellent order; and while they are driven by luminaries situated trillions, quadrillions, and perhaps more miles from our sun, they are nearly independent of our solar system—only dependent enough to be compelled to submit to slight repulsions of the planets and sun. Their eccentric orbits may be explained from the fact that they merely seek strata of light suited to their densities, and are repulsed by the direct and reflected light of the sun and planets.

If philosophers' opinions are correct at present, it is a mystery how these comets can pass through our system without being attracted to the sun or planets, without attracting some of the planets and carrying them off, and thus producing a general disaster among the heavenly bodies. Consequently, some suppose them to be mere vapors, or nebulous matter; while others assert that, if such were the fact, they approach so close to the sun, they would be dissipated or burned up. Neither hypothesis is true, for the sun is not a mass of liquid fire. It has one of the most equable, pleasant, invigorating, and glorious temperatures of any sphere in our solar system; and, instead of destroying, prolongs life and happiness forever. Fire, combustion, or ignition, is not an element any more than gunpowder, nitro-glycerine, or other explosives, and deserves to be stricken from the number of elements, and light substituted in its stead. Light is a producer; ignition, fire, and combustion, and also heat and cold, are destroyers. They are all quite different.

If these large comets have no existence only as vapors or will-o'-the-wisps, then there are no planets or heavens above; all that we see is a mere delusion of the brain, and the tomb must soon engulf us all, for want of a heaven in which to resurrect us. But such is not the truth; the heavens are visible to us, and, as sure as we live, move and breathe, we must and will be resurrected from the dead to them, and there rewarded according to our deeds.

Astronomy is a science of the most profound nature, and as yet is quite imperfectly under-

6

stood. God's wisdom and omnipotence are embraced within its precincts. He has confounded the wisdom of the wise in various ways. Our wisdom is merely foolishness compared to His; yet much can still be learned of His ways and laws. The philosophy I have advanced is true, and the motions of the heavenly bodies prove it; reason approves it, and then it has the sanction of the Bible and Christ, and sooner or later must become the basis of all true astronomy. I cannot, here, pursue it in detail, from the fact that I write without even a single copy of any work on astronomy, and have not read any since leaving school, upwards of twenty-five years ago; consequently, I would subject myself to numerous errors and criticisms, and may have done so already. I give merely the outlines, and, with what assistance others will give me, I promise to substantiate my philosophy. The details of it I will leave to others more learned than myself.

But this one fact is a matter of certainty:—Light is a grand, powerful, and glorious element, that supports the heavenly bodies and drives them in their orbits and on their axes. Philosophers can study and ascertain its nature with but little difficulty. They must first ascertain the true equator of the sun, then its poles, and then the position of our earth relative to its equator and poles; then the motions of the planets must be carefully noted, with all due regard to their annual and diurnal parallaxes, and the task is accomplished.

If the movements of the planets belonging to our solar system do not prove my philosophy on the supposition of the stronger light issuing from the equatorial regions of the sun, then try it on the supposition that it issues with equal power and revolves in all directions alike; for reason teaches that it is impossible for the sun, moon and stars to hang in a void space without any support. Newton's theory of nice equilibrium was quite learned enough for his day, but is entirely too rickety for the present. There is no other element to sustain them but light; and if the heavens are not supported by light, then they are without support.

But God created them with the utmost wisdom. Behold, what wisdom He has displayed in the creation of man, and the animals, and even the little insects and corals! and then answer if it is probable that He has created His own habitation, the heavens, in a manner which makes it subject to wreck or disaster. Not by any means. He has created the heavens for His own honor, and for the enjoyment of His angels; and will finally resurrect all the mortality of earth, whether rational or irrational, to them.

The heavens are as strong as an arch. If a power sufficient could be applied to them, the result would prove such to be the truth. All the planets are at certain places because no other is adapted to their density; and so of the sun and the fixed stars, all are at their proper places, and force each other there, and thus form a net-work of architecture through eternity.

How light emanates, or the cause of its issuing, from the sun, is a profound mystery. The sun is to our solar system just what the heart is to the corporeal body, only more so. We have life within us, but cannot tell why, other than God wills it so; so we know the sun gives light, but we do not know why, other than God made it so. Man cannot understand his own system, not even the little ants. The heavens are before him, yet he is confounded and forced to acknowledge his inferiority, and that he has his existence on an inferior planet. He sees and knows that he is not in his proper sphere, and casts his eyes heavenward for a better one. In this he will not be disappointed, for in heaven there is peace, love, happiness, and life eternal, for all. The strife, pain, desire, misery, and death, which characterize this earth, are there unknown. All the rest of the heavenly bodies are of the most delightful temperature, and, instead of destroying life, prolong it indefinitely. But the climate of the sun is the most pleasant, cheerful, and invigorating, of all; there the tree and fountain of life probably exist.

The planets, with the exception of this earth, are all as clean and neatly polished, by the sweeping light of the sun, as refined gold, and are just as clean and pure as the sun's rays. An angel might truly inhabit them and worship God through all eternity without having a stain or speck on his snow-white garments, because the sun's rays are grand polishers and beautifiers; hence angels are models of beauty and goodness. This would have been the condition of the earth if it had not been for the transgression of God's holy and just laws. It received a curse from God, and one of His vials of wrath was poured out on it in the shape of our atmosphere, which destroyed its peace, its beauty, its holiness, its life eternal, and caused it to be forsaken of God and the angels. We shall see presently that it is the proximate cause of all the ills of this earth, and that peace and life would forever reign if not prevented by the strife and changes produced by it. Moses says that all was good in the beginning, and, as we have no information of any curse existing against any of the planets except this earth, it must be taken for truth that all are yet good, with the one exception. Consequently, it may well be asserted that our atmosphere, or one of like nature, does not exist on any other celestial body. Certain compounds may exist there of similar appearance to it, but they are not of the same destroying nature, but quite the reverse; and instead of destroying life and begetting want and misery, prolong it indefinitely, and beget independence and endless joy and happiness.

All the planets are inhabited by superior beings, and so is the sun inhabited by a high order of beings, probably by Christ and his elect, as he was continually admonishing his apostles and disciples that they were to become the children of light. Many philosophers will here say that they would be burned up; but not by any means. Light is an element; fire is a destroyer that does not exist aside from this earth. An individual, like us, might safely stand on the sun, if otherwise adapted for the experiment, and not a hair of his head or a particle of his body would be singed. He might also pass through the centre of this earth, aside from volcanic burnings near its surface, and not be singed in the least. He would in neither instance experience the least unpleasantness from heat or cold, because they are merely properties of the atmosphere. This will be more fully explained in the next chapter.

Philosophers have made, and are still mak ing, discoveries relative to the exterior appearance of the planets. It is affirmed by them that some of the planets—Mars, for instance—have seas, inlets, and land, as this earth. Without doubt, Mars and all the other planets are beautifully diversified in their surfaces, so as to be exquisitely and even enchantingly interesting and pleasing, but it is not probable that that this is caused or made so by water and land. Moses says there was a time when "God had not caused it to rain upon the earth," and, in substance, that the plants and herbs were before they grew. Such must be the condition of the other planets. There are no seasons of heat, cold, clouds, rain, &c., upon them, because there is no atmosphere to cause such phenomena. Wherever a compound of oxygen and nitrogen, as our atmosphere, exists, there sorrow, strife, pain, and death, reign. Such do not exist in the heavenly bodies, if we are to believe the Bible. Even here on this earth, God could transform it into a paradise by pouring out on it a vial of the "water of life," or by planting the "tree of life" upon it; but this is not His purpose. The creatures of earth are too low and degraded to live forever; hence it is His purpose to reform and regenerate us all through death and the resurrection, according to our works, into a high and exalted condition in heaven. As it is written, "Eye hath not seen, nor ear heard, neither have entered into the heart of man, the things which God hath prepared for them that love Him."

These facts, however, do not prove that the planets, or even the sun, are not invested with the most beautiful scenery. They are all probably so invested, and are not a dull monotony. Angels are not mere insipid, mournful, and taciturn beings, but possess tastes for variety and pleasure as well as mankind: and we may expect to recognize our departed progenitors, relatives and friends in heaven, just precisely as we do on this earth; only, instead of finding them in want, desire, and misery, we will find them in affluence, independence, joy, and life eternal, as their works have deserved; but all rewarded with a hundred-fold more glory and abundance than they expected. Hence all is love, peace, and joy; for God has dealt nobly and bountifully with all. He has pleased the sinner and the righteous. To whom little was given, little was required; to whom much was given, much was required. Even the hypocrites and murderers would naturally have chosen the very positions assigned them, degraded as they are, because such are adapted to their natures and propensities. The tree and fountain of life is there free and accessible to all, and therefore death cannot reign over any.

It makes not the least difference that some planets do not revolve swiftly on their axes, so as to give short days and nights; they are not the subjects of heat and cold as our earth. There is sufficient light on all the planets from some luminary. The heavens are all illuminated in the most refulgent manner. The inhabitants of Jupiter and Saturn, though hundreds of millions of miles farther from the sun than we, are in the most agreeable and delightful temperature, unless they are perchance surrounded with a boisterous atmosphere like our earth—which cannot be the case, unless they are laboring under the displeasure of God. Moses forbade that idea when he said that God saw that it was good. All was good when created, but, as before observed, the earth has been accursed of God that insubordination might be punished and offenders regenerated.

As to the composition of the heavenly bodies, except the earth, it would be vain in man to speak. It may be affirmed, however, that they are composed of matter of some nature, and even of a very fine, or what we would term a precious nature. St. John, in his description of the New Jerusalem in the 21st chapter of Revelations, mentions some of these materials, which are very fine and precious, and much to be desired. Without doubt some of the heavenly bodies are of the most splendid description, far excelling our conception. Even our earth—this dusty, muddy, filthy, disagreeable globe of ours—if not subjected to the storms and strife of its atmosphere, would become as neat and clean as the sunbeams of heaven: they, in their flight and friction on it, would soon polish it as neatly as refined gold. Its water would sink by gravitation, as there would be no atmosphere to absorb it, and obscure the sunbeams, and cause rain; and it would also become solid, as glass or diamond. Thirst, pain, desire, hunger, decay, death, &c., are caused proximately by the air.

Heaven is not a breathing world like this. These breathing convulsions, or struggling between life and death, between heaven and earth, do not exist there. There life is glorious, perfect, and eternal. Mankind draw their notions of heaven from the visible objects of earth, and it may seem impossible to some that they could live without breathing; yet God teaches us this to our eyes, for we see creatures and animals living without breathing. Man's conceptions of heaven are derived too much from earthly objects. When he praises God by speaking or singing, he does so by reference to these objects; hence he is led away into idolatry.

As to the particular nature of angelic life and our heavenly Creator, we must be content to wait till God in His mercy and power shall develop the same to us in the resurrection;—that is a matter beyond human conception if even seen. But from the developments of their works in the starry heavens, and the sublime wisdom and power displayed in their creation and motions, it is patent to all that their existence is glorious and sublime. We may also safely conclude that our future state in heaven will far excel anything we now expect, if we but do right and respect God and His just laws. The Bible teaches this doctrine. John the Baptist was, without doubt, a very powerful and great man, yet Christ said the least in heaven was greater than he. St. John in Revelations speaks of "angels" and "powerful angels." Christ speaks of "life" and "life more abundantly"; he speaks of "damnation', and "damnation the greater." It may, therefore, be very properly inferred that the character and grades of happiness and glory of the angels of heaven must be different, and apportioned according to their merits or demerits. These works will speak for themselves; no witnesses will be necessary. Our works and deeds, whether they be good or evil, will be placarded on us as indelibly as the mark of Cain, and with the same truth and certainty that like begets like, and that everything yields and brings forth after its own kind. Deception is thereby rendered impossible, and neither God nor the hosts in heaven can be deceived.

Heaven has abundant room for all. It is teeming with life everlasting, its joys are unbounded, and its happiness complete and all-enduring. It is irrational to believe that God would permit any being, however small or insignificant, to suffer and die in this world, without some grand purpose. This purpose is regeneration and the resurrection to heaven. In due time God will restore us and not only us, but every living creature of earth, whether rational as man, or irrational as the beasts, and possessing His spirit of life, to His eternal and happy throne in heaven, where He will reward them all as their works shall be. We may expect to meet there not only our departed relatives and friends, but also our horse, cow, dog, and other domestic animals and fowls, and all other creatures of this earth that have enjoyed life on earth. Many of us, no doubt, will meet these irrational creatures to our eternal shame for the barbarity and cruelty we have practised towards them while on earth. All the irrational creatures of earth must finally appear in heaven and enjoy its blessings. Moses says they were in the beginning pronounced good, and there is no substantial reason why they should not be so again.

If scriptural authority is required to prove the resurrection of the irrational creatures of this earth, such as beasts, birds, fishes, &c., it may be found in the fifth chapter of Revelations, where St. John, in speaking of what he saw in his vision of the throne of God, says:

"And every creature which is in heaven, and
on the earth, and under the earth, and such as
are in the sea, and all that are in them, heard
I saying, Blessing, and honor, and glory, and
power, be unto Him that sitteth upon the
throne, and unto the Lamb, forever and ever."
Such language, when corroborated by reason,
justice, and benevolence, should be decisive
of the question. These matters will present
themselves again when we come to examine
the evidence of the resurrection from the dead.

Let us not, therefore, be so selfish and cruel
as to fancy a small limited space and call it
heaven, and claim it exclusively for ourselves,
and condemn all other of God's creatures to a
fiery hell; but let us rather claim that God's
whole universe is heaven, and that it contains
ample room, enjoyment, and happiness, not
only for us and our particular friends, but for
our neighbor and all the creatures of this
world. This supposition is the more just,
righteous, and intellectual, and we are not by
any means thus impugning either the omnipotence, justice or benevolence of an impartial

God. He can amply reward or degrade us before His throne, and will do so, as our works and conduct in life deserve. "Every man's work shall be made manifest: for the day shall declare it, because it shall be revealed by fire; and the fire shall try every man's work, of what sort it is. If any man's work abide which he hath built thereupon, he shall receive a reward. If any man's work shall be burned, he shall suffer loss: but he himself shall be saved; yet so as by fire." (1 Cor. iii. 13–15.) Here, the fire alluded to is the splendor of heaven that will be exhibited to us in the resurrection, which will make manifest all our works, and prove them, whether they be good or evil. If the works are good, they will receive a chief reward; if bad, they will be burned, that is, discarded as unworthy of a great reward. The individual is saved, however, but suffers loss; which clearly proves that all will be saved in heaven, though many will suffer loss by imperfect and wicked works. This also proves that our future estate is built upon our works here on earth; and unless we have numerous good works to exhibit in the resurrection, our

7

existence and enjoyment in heaven will be meagre indeed.

The subject of rewards and punishments is frequently alluded to in the Scriptures, and St. John in the 14th chapter of Revelations locates this dreadful "hell" which he had preached to the people of earth; and he locates it in the presence of the holy angels and the Lamb, or before the throne of God. Christ, in his parable of Lazarus and the rich man, locates the rich man in the presence of Abraham and the angels, within talking distance. The words "impassable gulf" and "far off" are mere figures of speech denoting rank, which could not be bettered or altered. Thirst represents a consciousness of inferiority. This punishment consists of degradation and shame, and fire, &c., represent the consciousness of it. This matter will, however, be reserved for another chapter.

We will now proceed to take a view of the situation and condition of our earth, in doing which many of the subjects contained in this chapter will recur and again become the subject of comment.

CHAPTER III.

THE EARTH.

ITS CREATION—ITS FORM AND REVOLUTIONS—THE BEGINNING—ITS CURSE—CREATION OF MAN—STRIFE OF EARTH CAUSED BY OUR ATMOSPHERE—ALL THE ILLS OF EARTH ASCRIBABLE TO IT—FIRE —HEAT—COLD—STRIFE OF NATURE—NEW THEORY OF THE SEASONS—LIFE—DEATH—TRUE CONDITION OF THE EARTH AND ITS INHABITANTS—THEIR FALLEN CONDITION—THEIR EVIL NATURE —GOD'S IMPARTIAL ADMINISTRATION—NO SPECIAL PROVIDENCES —THE EARTH FORSAKEN OF GOD AND THE ANGELS—THE LAW OF GOD—CHRIST, HIS NATURE AND TEACHINGS—MISERIES OF EARTH AND THEIR CAUSE—FORMER MILLENNIUMS.

The Earth is a large globe or sphere, and is about twenty-five thousand miles in circumference and nearly eight thousand miles in diameter. The rotundity of the earth is proved by its shadow on the moon during an eclipse, and also by travellers performing journeys around it. It is affirmed by learned men that its diameter is greater on a line passing through it at the equator than at the poles, or from pole to pole. This causes it to be oblate or flattened at the poles. They explain this by asserting that it was once in a liquid or molten state, and that the earth's velocity in its diurnal revolution is and was greater at the equator than at the poles, thus causing a force that would extend it at the equator and contract it at the poles.

Moses says that in the beginning the earth was without form and void. This gives philosophers a wide range for speculation; but very probably when the earth was created it was in a liquid state, and most probably was gradually formed by the power of light from the sun. Mankind are too apt to imagine that fire is the chief agent of every great work. They ransack their brains to see if they cannot discover its agency or existence in every material work of God. The ancients claimed that God was a consuming fire.

The earth is said to revolve around the sun annually, in an elliptic orbit, at the distance of ninety-five millions of miles from it. It also turns on its axis once in twenty-four hours, causing day and night. These facts are so well established by astronomy that they need no further proof. The starry heavens demonstrate these important facts, and also that the earth is only a planet like some of the stars of the firmament. The fixed stars are trillions of miles from the earth, and it is hardly conceivable that they should perform a journey around the earth in twenty-four hours. Reason forbids the idea, and we must content ourselves with the received theory that the earth is one of the planets of the universal heavens, performing like offices and journeys as these, with the exception spoken of by Moses, namely, that it is accursed of God for man's trangression.

As to the materials of the earth, they are said to be fire, air, earth, and water. These are called the four great elements of the earth, and, of course, include the animal, vegetable, and mineral kingdoms. These several kingdoms are properties of earth, while heat, cold, animal life, and death, are properties of the air: they, however, are conjoined with the earth, as spiritual life is to animal life.

As to the origin of the heavens and the earth, it is a matter beyond conception. Eternity is incomprehensible. When, where, and by what

means, the Almighty created the heavens and
the earth is a profound and unsearchable mystery. Moses assigns them a beginning, but
man cannot conceive a time and state of affairs
when there was no beginning or creation of
the heavens and earth. The heavens and the
earth are the attributes of eternity, and it might
well be affirmed that there never was the time
when they did not exist. There is no contradiction in this assertion with the Mosaic account as recorded in the first chapters of Genesis. Moses, in speaking of the creation of the
heavens and the earth, had no reference to solar or lunar time as it is now used in the world.
He represents the earth as existing before the
sun, moon, and stars, gave forth their light, by
which we compute time. Also, in the 1st chapter of Genesis, he gives an account of the creation of man; he says they were created "male
and female," and also in God's "own image,"
and that they had dominion over the earth.
He also affirms that God blessed them, and
gave them "dominion over the fish of the sea,
and over the fowl of the air, and over every

living thing that moveth upon the earth." The phrase "man in our image" is quite comprehensive as used by Moses, and embraces not only male and female, but the whole human family, and cannot by any fair interpretation have the least reference to Adam and Eve. Earth was then in all its primeval purity, and was free from sin, strife, desire, pain, decrepitude, and death, and probably had so existed eternally. It had not then received its curse, and was the ideal of Paradise—was good, holy, just, happy, and suited for the enjoyment of angels, and even its Creator.

Now in the next chapter Moses gives another account of the creation of man, which was Adam and Eve. These two personages are entirely different from those spoken of by him in the first chapter, as I shall show hereafter that they were placed in the garden of Eden, which could not have been on earth, and were driven from the garden to till the ground, from whence Adam was taken. This, Moses asserts, was done for his transgression; which is highly reasonable and proper, for God in His mercy

would certainly not inflict suffering and punishment on any creature unless for the most
potent and just reasons. Moses, therefore,
only attempted to give an account of the world
since the days of Adam, and the probability is
that the whole narrative, which is so graphic,
is a mere figure or symbol, and that the events
represented occupied countless years and centuries.

Before the earth received its curse, peace
must have reigned on it, and consequently its
surface was not subject to strife, disaster, and
change. These changes result from the motions of the atmosphere, and for the most part
are very gradual. The Chinese wall, the pyramids of Egypt, and other works of man, are
known to have existed and withstood these mu-
tations for thousands of years, with but little
change in the surface of the earth near them.
All changes, dirt, filth, and impurities of this
earth. are due to the action of our atmosphere
in causing strife; but the pyramids of Egypt
and the Chinese wall prove that these changes
are very gradual. These works must yet be

ground to dust by the strife of the atmosphere. We must therefore admit that immense time has been occupied in causing these changes, and that Moses had no reference to time as now used by mankind; he was simply endeavouring to teach spiritual matters by figures of speech, and therefore had resort to things of earth.

Geologists advance various theories respecting the formation of the earth. Some contend for an aqueous origin; that is, that water predominated, and that the earthy matter, as rocks, soils, minerals, &c., are the offspring of water. Others contend that the earth was originally in a liquid state caused by heat, and has been gradually cooling down; that fire predominates at the central portion of the earth, causing the phenomenon of the surface: this is called the igneous theory. They are mere theories advanced to explain the inequalities of the earth's surface, its formations, strata, dislocations, &c. The earth has never been penetrated very low or far beneath its surface, and the mysteries beneath are and

must remain mysteries more profound than
those above. Those above have the advantage
of light, while those beneath have not.

It cannot be contended that God in His infinite power and wisdom would need either the
agency of fire or water in constructing a world,
or that either of them are the chief agents of
his vast creation. It would have been just as
easy for Him to have used rubies, polished
gold, or emeralds, as fire, water, dirt, or other
substances appearing in its composition. It
would have been just as easy for Him to have
so organized man, and the creatures of earth,
that they would have been holy and happy
creatures, exempt from strife, pain, sin, desire,
hunger, thirst, disease, and death. But this is
not the case, and the very fact that it is not
is highly suggestive that there is something
wrong in man and the creatures of earth.

It would be highly absurd to suppose that
this earth has a magazine of fire at its centre,
and possesses the elements of its own destruction. There are some few phenomena that
philosophers cite as sustaining such a theo-

ry; one of these is the rolling or waving sensations produced by earthquakes. Some allege
that the surface of the earth is a mere crust or
integument, covering a fiery, molten mass beneath; that this crust is not very deep, and
becomes more of a fluid the farther we recede
from the surface; and that when the molten
mass below is disturbed, it causes upheavals
and the rolling or waving sensations felt during earthquakes. If this molten mass exists
there, their philosophy would be good; but
that is an assertion which no philosopher can
establish. It admits of no demonstration, and
is besides contrary to reason, and impugns the
benevolence and wisdom of God. Besides,
these rolling sensations experienced during
earthquakes could as well be produced by the
atmosphere being forced into or between the
strata of earth or layers of rocks, and by the
steam of volcanoes, as by the molten mass
supposed to exist below. Once set the supposed igneous fluid in motion, when would its
motions cease? In case the motion is produced by the atmosphere, it would cease as

quick as it could escape through the fissures
of the earth—which accords with the truth in
such cases.

There is, no doubt, much combustible matter within the bowels of the earth, but not
enough to effect its destruction even if it were
ignited. It can only be ignited by the atmosphere, and as the atmosphere does not extend
very deep, or penetrate the earth's surface
very far, no great calamity will ever befall the
earth. Volcanoes may destroy small areas, but
no great portion of the earth can be affected by
them, or by earthquakes. The combustible
materials of the earth and the atmosphere, if
brought in contact and then ignited by fire,
would be insufficient to accomplish the earth's
destruction. Animal and vegetable life would,
however, be extinguished, corruption banished, and the earth purified for a higher enjoyment and order of beings. This will not be
done, however; for such as it is, it is just as
God wishes it. Moses informs us that God destroyed the creatures of the earth once, except
what He preserved through Noah and his ark;

and how easy to have effected the annihilation of Noah and those saved in the ark, if it was His pleasure that the world and its inhabitants should be remodelled! The truth is, it exists here for the most wise and beneficent purposes, the chief of which are to teach lessons of adoration, repentance, humility, justice, love, charity, &c., and for regeneration into heaven.

But let the earth be made when and however it may, and be composed of whatever it may, the chief cause of all the ills that its mortality is subjected to exists in our atmosphere. This elastic and transparent substance surrounding the earth, as the learned inform us, is composed of oxygen and nitrogen. There are some few other substances that enter into its composition, but they are, perhaps, only its impurities. Our atmosphere cannot extend very far above the surface of the earth, on the average not over forty-five miles. It possesses weight and great elasticity. Heat and cold, also, are properties of the atmosphere, and I affirm cannot anywhere exist unless the body or object is subjected to, or under the influence of, the atmosphere. The atmosphere penetrates and exerts an influence on the earth to a great depth—the deeper in the earth the less, until its influence is entirely annihilated; and so of the horizon above, the higher you go, or farther from the earth's surface, the less its influence, till you reach a distance of forty-five miles at the equator, or from thirty-nine to forty-two miles at the poles of the earth, when it entirely ceases. We are thus buried in a deep ocean of air, and live and can only enjoy carnal life in it. Without its limits and influence, no mortality can survive for any considerable period. While its properties sustain animal life for a season, it carries within it heat and cold, or heat and cold result from the action of the sun and other heavenly bodies on it; and these are the producers or generators of animal and vegetable life, disease, desire, pain, hunger, death, &c.

The seasons of the year—as spring, summer, fall, and winter, or seasons of heat and cold—are generally ascribed to the heat of the sun. Astronomers contend that the sun is a fiery mass, and imparts heat to the earth by its rays; that in winter the rays of the sun fall obliquely on the earth, owing to the inclination of the earth's axis, and the fact that it does not shine on the earth, or particular part of it subject to winter, as long in winter as in summer, and consequently cannot impart as much heat. If the sun possesses the heat ascribed to it by them, their philosophy, of course, is true. But the reader will remember that I have already denied this, as being at variance with the benevolence and goodness of the Creator and the uniformity of His laws; and I must again be allowed to assert that heat and cold are properties of our atmosphere, and can exist only in it and by its influence; and that our air is an element belonging exclusively to the earth and does not (with its poisonous absorptions, strife, changes, disease, and death) exist around the heavenly bodies, spreading its evils over them.

The seasons of the year result from the action of the sun and other celestial bodies on the atmosphere. Its chief property is cold

and the cold of the earth would be insupportable if it was not counteracted by the influ
ence of the celestial bodies. These impart
heat to our atmosphere, not by any intrinsic
heat they possess, but by penetrating the
same and making war upon them, causing
strife and friction among its particles, and thus
producing the heat the world enjoys. Now,
as we ascend upwards the specific gravity and
density of the atmosphere diminishes; the
component parts are more sparse and this
strife and friction become less, and consequently the cold increases and the heat diminishes. At the distance of five miles from the
surface, even at the equator, it is immensely
cold; at the distance of ten miles from the
surface animal life would instantly be extinguished by cold, because the strife and friction produced by the rays of the sun and heav
enly bodies would be so greatly diminished
as to produce little heat. However, as strife
ceases peace would reign, and at the distance
of ten miles from the surface there would be
no clouds, the sun would shine in sublime bril-

liancy, the motion of the atmosphere would scarcely be perceptible, and we would almost be ready to exclaim that peace reigned; but no true peace reigns in our atmosphere; although strife is not perceptible to us, yet it exists as far as it extends. The air at the distance of ten or even six or seven miles from the earth would be too rare and light for even a falcon or sparrow to fly in; hence, if by any means they could be forced that high, they would fall down to the earth as dead; sound would also cease to a great degree; while the report of a cannon that could be heard twenty miles at the earth's surface, could not probably be heard one mile if made ten miles above it.

. But the reader will say that this does not explain the causes of the seasons; but it does, if you will but apply the rules that philosophers commonly teach. That is, first apply the rule that the centrifugal force at the earth's surface is much greater at the equator than at the poles, and consequently that by its force and tension the greatest bulk of the earth is under the equator: now, if this centrifugal

8

force had power to force the greater part of the cohesive matter of earth under the equator, how much more power has it to force our elastic atmosphere there! Consequently, I have once affirmed that the atmosphere is much deeper and heavier and more dense at the equator than at the poles of the earth. If the reader will accept this position as true, he may then explain the causes of winter, summer, spring, and fall, just as our philosophers, to-wit, by the inclination of the earth's axis, causing the bulk of the atmosphere (and bulk of strife and heat) to lie at the tropic of Cancer, or twenty-three and a half degrees north of the equator, at the summer solstice; and to lie at the tropic of Capricorn, or the same distance south of the equator, at the winter solstice.

Now, if I am correct as to my theory of heat and cold, animal and vegetable life cannot exist at the north and south poles, from the fact that the atmosphere is too light; so much of it is thrown under the equator by the rotary motion of the earth that it has not sufficient depth and density to sustain either animal or vegetable life. Everything, no doubt, would look very quiet and peaceable, for there is but little strife in nature at those points.

Of course, the sun's rays by the agency of the air make war on the earth's surface and everything that is impure, causing strife, friction, and heat, amidst their impure particles; and this strife, heat, and friction, also result if, by the inclination of the earth's axis, they strike the earth obliquely. The sun's rays do not possess heat, and heat and cold do not exist except by medium of the atmosphere. With a powerful double convex lens the sun's rays can be made to produce a powerful heat, but it is caused by great friction of the particles of the air. It will not produce heat in a vacuum, or place from which the air is excluded. Just as far as air extends, there heat may be produced. Some substances also conduct heat, as the metals, &c.; but heat cannot be created solely by the properties of the atmosphere. It cannot exist at the centre of the earth nor above our atmosphere. The snow-clad moun-

tains near the equator are living witnesses that
the sun's rays do not possess heat; otherwise
they could not retain ice on them all the year
round. The theory has been that the earth is
very hot at its centre; that the temperature
gradually diminishes as the surface is approached, and that heat is not conveyed up to
these high peaks from the earth owing to their
altitude and peakedness.

Cold is a property of the air, and so is heat,
and aside from it all is of the most equable
and delightful temperature, giving and pro-
moting life eternally. Cold and heat cannot
impart pain to the senses except by the atmosphere, while light is life-giving and life-pro-
moting; hence life is eternal aside from this
earth. Once admit that heat results from friction and strife produced by the penetration of
the sun's rays and light of the other celestial
bodies on our atmosphere, and that the greatest density of the atmosphere is thrown under
the sun by the rotary motion of the earth, and
we then can explain the seasons according to
the rules of philosophy as now taught.

I will remark, before dismissing this subject, that the barometer is by no means an accurate indicator either of altitude, or density of the atmosphere. It may attain accuracy in some measure, but, from various causes, such as climatic phenomena, rarefaction by heat near the earth's surface, &c., is not perfect.

We will now examine the properties of our atmosphere, its abrasions and other effects upon the surface of the earth, and we will find that carnal life, strife, sin, pain, desire, hunger, thirst, disease, misery, and death, result from its action on the earth and its creatures. As to its composition, it has been remarked already that it is composed of nitrogen and oxygen, and some few other substances which are probably absorbed by it and might be called impurities. The exact proportion of these constituents need not be stated for the purposes of this work. The air is transparent, possessing specific gravity, together with great elasticity and mobility. The application of small force will compress it or set it in motion. Heat, by its rarefying quality, is the great source of the motions of the atmosphere. The atmosphere also possesses, when in motion, great absorptive powers; when still, it possesses none. It is continually absorbing the moisture and gases of the earth and sea. It also absorbs the moisture from the bodies of men and animals — not only from the surface of their bodies, but it enters into their lungs and stomachs, and prosecutes its work there. This action of the air on the skin, stomach, lungs, and bowels, is the immediate cause of hunger, thirst, desire, pain, death, &c. The air is the immediate cause of animal and vegetable life; it begets heat, cold, and the seasons; it absorbs vapors and produces rain; this, combined with heat and sunshine, begets vegetation; vegetation sustains animal life. There could be no animal or vegetable life on earth if the air did not exist on it. As the air produces vegetation, it also produces desire, &c. and hence animal life results. Animal life could not exist without it for any considerable length of time. This is true even with the fishes and inhabitants of the sea, though they require a much less portion of air than the land animals.

The water itself is impregnated with the atmosphere, and is indebted to it for its liquidity and mobility; in other words, if there was no air in the water it would cease to flow, and would become a solid substance similar in appearance to glass. The reader may wish proof of this; if so, Moses in the 1st chapter of Genesis corroborates it, and so also does scientific experiment. Moses writes, "And the Spirit of God moved upon the face of the waters." The word "face" here evidently signifies surface, and from this very assertion of holy writ it is not by any means unreasonable for us to suppose that the sea and waters of the earth were once a solid, as clear, pure, and neat, as polished glass, and that they probably covered the whole face of the earth. The earth was not then surrounded with this atmosphere, and consequently had suffered no violence or strife, and must have been inhabited by a higher and nobler race of beings than it is now. This accords with the idea heretofore advanced, that "man," or the race of beings spoken of by Moses in the 1st chapter of Genesis, was not the same as Adam and Eve spoken of in the 2nd chapter. The first were an angelic people, and had great powers, among which was locomotion and ability to live in and traverse the light of heaven, from one part of the heavens to another; consequently. they were ordered away before any curse was pronounced on Adam or the earth.

The Bible expressly affirms that man (or our first parents, Adam and Eve) and the earth received a curse from God ; observation also fully confirms it, and it may safely be affirmed that the earth and its creatures have been greatly affected by it and an entire change made. The change was from pure, holy, independent and happy angels, dwelling and enjoying themselves on an emerald sea, where there was neither pain, heat, cold, hunger, thirst, desire, misery, sorrow, tears, nor death—where there was no filth, sin, or corruption—where the love of their Creator smiled upon and enlightened their homes,—to the filth, corrup-

tion, sin, desire, misery, and death, existing
on the earth, which we see, and the world has
seen since it has been under the displeasure
of Almighty God.

Instead of being a sea of elysian joy and
happiness, the earth with its elements is now
one vast whirlpool of destruction, first giving
animal and vegetable life, and then destroying
it. It might truly be called the wine-press of
God's wrath.

The air we breathe is impure, so is the water we drink and the food we eat. These are
all substances which, though necessary to sustain animal life, carry within them, and are
productive of pain, misery, disease, decrepitude, and finally death to all living creatures.
The earth's surface is continually undergoing
a change, however imperceptible. The things
of to-day will not be to-morrow. One generation appears, and swiftly passes away to give
place to another, while still another and
another succeed each other. This is true both
of the animal and vegetable kingdoms. The
mighty oak of the forest is not sufficient to

withstand the storms and vicissitudes of earth.
These changes are so potent that even the gra-
nite rocks of the hills and mountains become
affected by them, and exhibit signs of change
and decomposition. Wherever our atmosphere
can find an entrance, there it performs its
work, accomplishing at times violently, and at
times slowly and imperceptibly, its destined
purpose.

The atmosphere is, without doubt, the agent
of all changes on the earth.   It employs other
agents, as heat, cold, water, fire, earth, &c.; but
it rules and directs them.   It owes its power
to the sun and lights of heaven.   Abstract
these and it is powerless. The rays of the sun
and the light of the heavenly bodies penetrate
our atmosphere, causing strife, friction, and
heat.   This heat rarefies it, and as it becomes
rarefied it is displaced by a volume of air more
dense, either from above, below, or laterally;
this arises from its great elasticity and mobility.   The air as it becomes heated and rarefied
at the equator is superseded and displaced by
the denser air from the poles or from above,

but principally from lateral directions. This causes wind and sometimes violent hurricanes, by which the works of man, and even the monarchs of the forest, tremble and fall, and are left a wreck of ruin. When in more gentle mood, the air is continually absorbing and carrying up vapors, gases, and poisonous particles, from the surface of the earth, the vapors become condensed by the electrical power of heat and cold, and fall again to the earth in the form of rain. This process is continually going on, and gives animation to the vegetable kingdom. The poisonous properties absorbed by the atmosphere are carried about in it, and are hurled even into the lungs and stomachs of the breathing, eating and drinking creatures of the world, causing disease, decay and death.

It cannot be expected that I should in a work like this discuss the principles of aërology or climatology to any considerable extent. That science is yet in its infancy, and but imperfectly understood by the most learned; yet I may be allowed to say that much of its phenomena can be well understood and explained

if our learned men will set themselves to the
task. It will, perhaps, require the observation
of centuries to render it anything like perfect;
but as science progresses, and the world becomes more populous, it will be a matter of
more importance to them than to us to understand this science. Food with our posterity
will, perhaps, be a matter of much more con-
cern than to us; and if we can by any reasonable exertions of our own furnish them the
means of ascertaining excessive wet, drouth,
heat and cold, or of good and light crop years,
our christian duty imperatively requires that
we should do so.

From what I have already advanced, the
reader may infer that my opinion is that the
climatic changes of the earth are not altogether
ascribable to the mountain ranges and eleva-
tions of the earth's surface above the level of
the sea, and the rotary motion and inclination
of the earth's axis, but to the movements of
the heavenly bodies, less or more distant, than
that the sun has much influence over our climate. This position, if correct, can be proven

only by actual observation through a long period of time, and a faithful record and comparison of events. The observation should be general and careful.

The air has caused all the changes we witness on earth. It not only effects changes on the earth, but it enters at times and places far beneath its surface; there it ignites combustible materials, causing a change and destruction by that means; at times, this change, or apparent destruction of matter, prepares the way for the entrance of water into the fiery mass; this precipitates the water into steam, which produces volcanoes and earthquakes. Wherever air can enter it effects changes.

It might very properly be asked in this place, why or for what reason mankind and the living and breathing creatures of this world were surrounded by, or submerged in, this deadly element of strife. There is reason for it, and Moses was undoubtedly correct when he ascribed it to man's transgression.

We know that air is very necessary to animal and vegetable existence, and that without it they cannot exist, yet, however pure the air we breathe, the water we drink, the food we eat, and however comfortable our shelter and raiment, yet man and all living creatures of earth must perish and die from the effects of the atmosphere. There is no way or manner by which to escape death for any. Solemn as the thought may be, *all must die;* for it is a law of heaven. Physicians may select the most salubrious air, the choicest and most nutritious food, the purest and most wholesome water, and the most comfortable and desirable raiment and shelter, and administer these blessings to the mortal possessing the most robust and well organized constitution; yet that mortal must sicken, decay, and die, in a few fleeting years. The high, the low, the rich, the poor, the weak, the strong, the wise, the unwise, are all doomed alike to decay, disease, and death, under its powerful agency. It is an element from which there is no escape. It is the flaming sword, spoken of by Moses, which turned every way to keep the way of the tree of life.

The water of earth, that compound of hydrogen and oxygen, is another element of earth quite deleterious to animal life. It carries many impurities in it. All the evils of water result from the action of the atmosphere. Its fluidity is directly owing to the presence of the air in and upon it. It would neither have a single impurity in it, a stain about it, color, taste or smell—neither would it flow, but be as nice and hard as a diamond—if it were not for our atmosphere. It has decomposed it; and hence whatever is at present objectionable in water may be attributed to the air. And the same may be said of earthy matter: it was once as solid and as neat as polished glass; and if it protruded through the waters at all, as at present, it was the fit abode of angels, and varied the pleasures of ear'h during its primitive purity.

The filth, impurities, and corruptions, that now overspread the earth did not exist till the fall of Adam and Eve. The earth was then, or prior thereto, clad with the air; and this filth, corruption, decay and death, are the results.

Fire is said to be another powerful element of earth. We may well doubt that it is an element; but it has no existence beyond our atmosphere or its influence, and before the fall of Adam there was not a spark of it on earth, nor was any needed. I defy any philosopher to prove by any correct reasoning that fire exists in any of the heavenly bodies. Fire is one thing, the light of heaven quite another and different thing. Fire is the result of strife. Light is an element, just as earth, air, and water, and is the most powerful element of the heavens. It is capable of supporting the heavens and the earth, with all the weight philosophers attribute to them. It is creative in its nature, while fire decomposes and disorganizes. Light—this etherial light existing throughout the heavens—has its inhabitants, just as the earth, water, and air, have theirs. Though we cannot comprehend and carnally see these spiritual beings of light, and understand the nature of their existence, yet it by no means follows that they do not exist. They are not mere shadows, phantoms, or nonentities; but their works, exhibited in the heavens, show that they are powerful beings, capable of high attainments which are totally unknown to earth. They so far excel the inhabitants of earth, that man in his degradation cannot form any just or perfect ideas concerning them. The idea of powerful beings existing, and performing such wonderful works as the heavens present to our view, in an invisible, noiseless, and unobserved manner, is something astounding to humanity. That such is the fact nature teaches by all her works, both of sea and land, and by heaven and earth.

Mankind has in all ages had a mania as to fire. The ancients claimed that God was a "consuming fire"; and there is only one rational way of accounting for this mania, and that is, that this earth has once been illuminated by the passage, in its orbit, of some powerful celestial body more luminous than the sun, causing a millennial peace, during which the ancients witnessed the presence of angels, and heard the Gospel of Peace and Truth

9

preached. We will defer notice of this for a future chapter; but this mania must have originated in that manner. Why philosophers should assert that the sun is a mass of liquid fire is unaccountable. It is certainly not because fire emits a faint light when burning in our atmosphere. Do they imagine that our fire—the burning of wood and combustible materials—if placed beyond the limits of our atmosphere, could emit any light? or could it if in full blast, be even seen? If the reader will permit me to advance my opinion, I will assert that it could not emit any light, or be seen on earth. Ignition or combustion is one thing, and light another. Ignition is of earth, transitive and sensual; while light is of heaven, durable, all-powerful, and spiritual. A mere flame or firebrand would not illuminate the vast etherial space of heaven, but it requires the power of spiritual light, as exerted eternally, and with the utmost precision and regularity by the Creator.

Electricity is a phenomenon of the air, and only exists in the air or by its action. This is a powerful agent, and at times performs some unpleasant offices. However, it is beneficial in purifying the atmosphere. It condenses vapors and causes rain; it also condenses the dust and calcareous matter carried up in the air by absorption, and even melts them and throws them again to the earth in the form of rocks or meteoric stones. Some say these stones come from the destruction of other planets; but this is sheer nonsense. Electricity also burns up or decomposes the poisonous particles of matter floating in the atmosphere, and renders it pure. Sometimes its workings seem providential, or the result of the direct interposition of Providence; but such cannot be the truth. Providence governs by the most impartial and unerring laws.

This element, fire, is one of strife; it exists only by strife, and cannot exist without it. The Bible and reason also teach that heaven is peace, and consequently this fire of earth cannot and should not have existence or place there. It might, therefore, safely be affirmed, that, if a man was otherwise adapted, he might safely inhabit the sun, as not a hair of his head would be singed or injured, though he was in the flesh as now; of course, none can go there in the flesh, because it is at enmity with God, and doomed to die on earth.

The attraction of gravitation is also an evil of earth, as it hinders our powers of locomotion or change of place. In some aspects of the case, it may be a blessing; but if man and the animals were otherwise in their proper and primeval spheres of action, this law of gravitation would be a great evil and hindrance. The mighty animals of the sea rise from its depths and slime and move through its waters, and the birds of the air fly through it with great velocity; but man and the animals are confined by gravitation to the slime and filth of the earth. "Man" (and Job might have said the same of all the creatures of earth) "is of few days, and full of trouble."

The question here presents itself, why are these troubles? why these ills? Let us examine these questions for a few moments, for without doubt there are just reasons for their existence, and for the present condition of affairs on earth, if we could but trace them to their proper source.

It is evident that the atmosphere, water, food, &c., of earth were so designed by God himself, and that our present existence is just as He desires it. Our conduct, however, may be just the reverse, as He has given us a will of our own, and laws for our moral and spiritual government, just as He gives to His children in heaven. A higher and more noble life and state of affairs is clearly depicted to us in the firmament of heaven; our inferiority and degradation is visible and apparent. And again, let me ask, why so? Can it be that this earth is a nursery, or the womb of Eternity? We should be happy to believe that doctrine, but the Bible as well as reason forbid it; and there is no way to escape the conviction that mankind and the creatures of this world are undergoing punishment, reformation, and regeneration, and that the earth is the place designated by our Creator for that purpose; that we are violators of God's holy laws, and

are placed here for such violation; that we are
not suffering for Adam and Eve's conduct, but
for our own, of like nature. Our first parents
were condemned in the garden of Eden—which
is a mere figure of heaven, or some part of it—
and were driven out to earth. Christ taught
Nicodemus that no man hath ascended up to
heaven, except he that came down from heav-
en. This proves that the present inhabitants
are also outcasts of heaven, and delivered over
to our arch-enemy—the Devil, Satan, serpent,
or flesh of the world—for works of atonement
and regeneration. Our regeneration is com-
pleted in carnal death, and we will again be
restored to heaven by the force and power of
the resurrection, and enjoy heaven according
to our works of repentance on earth.

Man is a compound of the spiritual and the
carnal. His spiritual nature is truth, love,
justice, &c., while his carnal nature is quite
the reverse. Our spiritual nature, which is
the true man, once existed in heaven; and
hereafter must continue there to exist in some
estate, either exalted or humble, as our works

shall determine. The spiritual nature is immortal, and therefore cannot or will not ever perish; our carnal bodies must die, for they and their passions are the great enemies of truth, justice, and righteousness. The spiritual nature of man is heavenly, exalted, holy, and righteous. It is continually admonishing us of heaven, and prompting us to deeds of love, charity, justice, and mercy; while the flesh is prompting us to deeds of wrong, sin, covetousness, oppression, folly, crime, and death.

The flesh is evil; it is one of the evils inflicted on earth, and we may well conclude that flesh, as it moves and exists by the Spirit of God on earth, cannot and does not exist in heaven, or anywhere else except on earth, and that when consigned to the tomb it will never be resurrected. Many, no doubt, entertain a different view of the subject from the fact that they interpret the Bible literally, as any other book, while the truths in most of its teachings are promulgated by parables, symbols, and figurative language. The fall of man was

without doubt announced in figurative language, and so of many of the events contained
in the Bible. We are bound to admit this, or
falsify the book itself; and when we can render it consistent and intelligible by resorting
to figurative construction, it is incumbent on
us to do so, rather than make its records of
events impossibilities or falsehoods by a literal construction. For this reason, I maintain
that Moses' description of the manner in which
he received the ten commandments is figurative of a former millennium, for it is improbable that the just and impartial God of the Universe should so far disregard His impartiality
as to advise and bless one nation and its rulers
and not the others. Such is at variance with
the general teachings of the Bible, such is at
variance with all just ideas of His omnipotence; for He could not appear on the earth
without every mortal creature recognizing the
fact; and, finally, Moses himself informs us
that the law existed at the beginning, when
Cain slew Abel, and even before sacrifices
were offered. From these considerations we

are forced to conclude that Moses' account of
his reception of the ten commandments is figurative, and so of many other of his writings;
they are mere figures of speech, but not intelligible now to us, or important.

Many believe that mankind will be resurrected after death and exist here on earth, and
live forever in a similar condition as they now
do. It seems hard for many of us to give over
this body of ours to death and destruction;
but, whether we will or not, such is the decree
of God. This disposition not to give over and
admit the destruction of the body—this mass
of flesh, blood, bones, &c.—arises from the fact
that man is not capable of discerning and
comprehending a better and higher existence.
The reader must not believe that I would commit him or her to the tomb, and deny the resurrection and a future enjoyment in heaven;
not by any means, for I contend that the resurrection extends to all mankind, the good and
evil; and not only mankind, but all the creatures of earth having the Spirit of God within
them. Life here is insignificant to that in

heaven. The bodies we now possess are just as insignificant to those we shall possess as the acorn is to the oak, and we will have no more need for our bodies in heaven than the oak of the forest has for the hull through which it germinated. Life here on earth is only the germ of our future existence, and death is the mere bursting forth into heaven and a heavenly existence. Once admitted into heaven's elysian joys, and we will be nurtured by the love and power of angels instead of the weakness of earth. We will then need no disordered flesh, no impure blood, no aching bones, no vitiated appetite, no frail sinews or muscles; but God in His providence will furnish us with a body, just as our merits shall deserve, that shall far eclipse our expectations. Therefore no one, however much he have degraded himself, need be afraid to make the exchange, for Christ says the least in heaven shall be greater than John the Baptist; and if we consider his merits, we need not fear a cheat in the exchange, however badly we may have acted. This body of ours is carnal, sens-

ual, earthly, and devilish; while the other, in
the eternal world, will be shorn of these weak-
nesses, and endowed with virtues and powers
with which we are now unacquainted—at least
all of us who may be found worthy.

The strife which pervades the elements of
earth also exists in man. There is war in his
organization; his complex existence is in a
state of strife, the good combatting the evil,
truth combatting error. Man has a vicious
nature in him, and there is nothing pure and
heavenly on earth except the Spirit of God
and the light of heaven. This Spirit of God
within us is pure, heavenly, righteous, and
holy, and is truth. The light we enjoy is
truth, and is likewise pure, holy, perfect, and
just, and is from heaven. The sight of men
and animals, this power of beholding corporeal objects on earth, and a few of the works
of the almighty Architect as delineated in the
nearest portion of the heavens, is spiritual,
and is the direct gift of the Creator. This eyesight or vision, though the gift of heaven, is
quite imperfect and obscured by the darkness

of earth. The earth, though lighted with the sunbeams of heaven, is, spiritually speaking, in darkness. We see and cannot comprehend. The sight and comprehension are both defect-ive, which proves man's degradation. Yet in this world of darkness enough vision is left to man to behold the wondrous extent, mechan-ism and magnificence of much of the heavens. His sight is more perfect than his reason or speech, for he is endowed with no thought suf-ficient to conceive and understand, or tongue to express, the grandeur and majesty of the scene.

Heaven in part is spread before our eyes, yet seeing we cannot comprehend its majesty. We cannot comprehend the mysteries of the heavens, nor is necessary that we should, or proper that we should. If we could, it would be ample evidence that a heavenly existence is but little superior to earth; while the very fact that these mysteries are incomprehensible to us, is the most convincing and conclusive proof that our future existence will be one of the most transcendent and sublime order, if

we shall but act worthily. This higher existence, to which we are so rapidly hastening, is
no vague or foolish surmise of the carnal mind,
but is a positive, true, and holy reality, and
one which will be developed and manifested
by the power of God in the resurrection of all
the creatures of earth, whether rational as man,
or irrational as the beasts, &c., in a short, a
very short time.

Without the light of heaven and the organs
of sight the heavens and earth could not endure. Light is sometimes refracted by the
elements and substances of earth, such as air,
water, and polished substances, so as to deceive; but if left to itself, with no disturbing
elements, it is always true. So also with the
spirit of man; if left free from disturbing in-
fluences and from temptation, it is always just.
The sight is obscured in many ways; but the
great obscurity called "spiritual darkness" in
the Scriptures, arises from the transcendent
splendor of heaven. The phenomenon of combustion or ignition, on earth, which we call
fire, and for which mankind have such a su-

perstitious horror, compared to the splendor of heaven, would look dark; if placed beyond our atmosphere, it would seem as a black speck or cloud, and would not illuminate in the least, so brilliant are the heavens beyond our atmosphere. This brilliancy begins at the earth's surface, and the farther you leave it the thinner the air becomes and the more resplendent become the sun's rays, till finally the air ceases and the heavens are illuminated with the most majestic grandeur—where there is neither cold, heat, pain, desire, hunger, thirst, tears, sorrow, nor death.

Our powers of sight are imperfect and often obscured by the rays of the sun. For illustration, suppose that an intelligent person should have been excluded from a view of the heavens by night till he was grown, but that he was only permitted to see the world and philosophize on it during the day. Tell him that there exists a vast system of architecture in the heavens besides the sun; and that it extends indefinitely and eternally into unbounded space, and that the same would be shown to him some night, what do you suppose would be his anxiety, and what his doubts? He would, perhaps, have about the same anxiety and patience that man has as to the reality of God's existence, and his own resurrection in heaven; and his doubts would be similar, and in fact should be greater, for he must depend on the truthfulness of man; while man has ocular demonstration of his heavenly abode, and nature teaches him, through all her works, his resurrection to the same. Take the same individual by night, when the heavens are unobscured by clouds, and point his sight to the heavens, and how sublime his thoughts, and how convincing the proof emanating from heaven itself! Mankind have but little need of a teacher when God himself reveals and teaches.

There is a view from the standpoint of life; this we now have. There is another view from the standpoint of death and the resurrection; this we must all soon have, when our vision will embrace things spiritually. The obscurity and darkness of earth will soon have vanished, and the light mankind so much desire will brilliantly illuminate the heavens, where an all-wise and all-powerful God, together with His angels and ransomed hosts of earth, will appear in unspeakable glory and power — where the redeemed shall no more experience neither pain, sorrow, hunger, thirst, desire, nor death; for they are free from the troubles of earth, and will reign forever. How different this splendor and glory to that of earth! Earth has but few joys, scarcely any without their price of toil, labor, and suffering; and how fleeting are these! Heaven's rewards and joys are without price, and can be attained with righteous works while here on earth. Heaven's joys are durable, earth's are fleeting and uncertain. Our joy is often abruptly turned to mourning. If we eat, we hunger again; if we drink, we thirst again. If we clothe ourselves and build houses to shelter ourselves against the rigors of the seasons, we soon find that time and the vicissitudes of earth demolish our fabrics, and they must be renewed. If we are in good health, we have no assurance that disease, disaster and death are not at our doors. If we labor and sow, we have no positive assurance that we shall reap. In truth, this world is one of change, and the measure of life is uncertain. "Man is of few days, and full of trouble." The whole mechanism of earth, as organized by the Creator, is specially designed to effect changes, repentance, and regeneration, through carnal death and the resurrection to a spiritual life in heaven. Every event militates against our sojourn on earth. The food we eat, the water we drink, the air we breathe, though necessary to animal life, yet have death and decay scattered in them. Many of us are poorly clad and sheltered, and we must soon depart. The earth bids us leave—God and the heavens invite us to come; and why should mankind fail to be prepared and ready for the journey?

The carnal nature of man is full of corruption, and is even more so than the elements of earth. It is the thing called *self*—which is figuratively called in the Bible, through respect to the higher nature of man, the old ser-

10

pent, Satan, Devil, &c.   It is antagonistic to truth, love, mercy, righteousness, justice, &c. What God commands, it forbids; what heaven dictates, it opposes; what justice requires, it dispenses with; what purity and holiness exacts, it declines.   Though made alive and existing only by the quickening power of the Spirit of God, as developed in the bodies of men and animals, yet it is at continual enmity with God and His holy laws. It seeks to allure from the path of duty; it seeks to deceive us, and prompts to a violation of God's laws; it even denies the existence of God, though trembling in the fear of His power. This principle (self) is blind; it knows not justice nor its own; it has no respect for the rights of others, and is continually at war with every principle of truth, right, justice, love, mercy, and everything that is heavenly.

What more need or can be said of the Devil, Satan, dragon, serpent, &c., mentioned in the Bible? According to the 12th chapter of Revelations, the dragon is on earth; and this is the principle called "self" by us, as it exists in

man and animals of the earth; that is, the carnality of earth represents him. That chapter
informs us that "there was war in heaven:
Michael and his angels fought against the
dragon; and the dragon fought and his angels, and prevailed not; neither was their
place found any more in heaven. And the
great dragon was cast out, that old serpent,
called the Devil, and Satan, which deceiveth
the whole world; he was cast out into the
earth, and his angels were cast out with him."

The above is good Bible proof that Satan is
on earth; but such terms as Satan, Devil, hell,
dragon, fire and brimstone, &c., are figures of
speech used in the Bible to denote the evil nature of man's earthly passions, and to denote
the remorse, shame and degradation that evil-
doers must be subjected to, in the resurrection, by the laws of heaven.

The 3d chapter of Genesis informs us that
Adam was sent forth to till the ground from
whence he was taken. So Adam and the dragon, Satan, or the Devil, became inhabiters of
the earth. It was the serpent that deceived

Adam and Eve; and they both are, without doubt, outcasts from heaven according to Moses, Christ, and St. John. The earth, therefore, certainly was accursed long before the fall of Adam, for it is highly improbable that God would furnish the serpent a paradise for his abode, and fallen man this world of strife and sin. There is nothing contradictory in the Mosaic account of the creation and fall of man to this opinion. The language of Moses is, "Cursed is" (not *cursed be*) "the ground for thy sake." St. Peter, in his second epistle, chapter second, in speaking of false teachers, says, "For if God spared not the angels that sinned, but cast them down to hell, and delivered them into chains of darkness, to be reserved unto judgment." Now in this language we have the express opinion of St. Peter as to the condition of mankind, and the true name and state of earth and its inhabitants. That we are the fallen angels reserved for judgment is clearly indicated, and the " chains of darkness" and "hell" clearly have reference to the earth.

Adam and all the creatures of earth were and are placed here on earth for violation of the laws of heaven, and are to undergo judgment for their deeds done in the body. This earth represents the forbidden fruit of the Bible, and is yet forbidden to the angels of heaven. It is the tree of the knowledge of good and evil. St. James, in speaking of the effects of envy and strife, says (see 3d chapter), "For where envying and strife is, there is confusion and every evil work." Again he says, "This wisdom descendeth not from above, but is earthly, sensual, devilish." Here we have his opinion as to the condition of earth. This earth is the only place where evil exists, or is for a moment suffered to exist. Moses says that "God saw that it was good," meaning the creation of heaven and earth. The angels of heaven could not acquire this knowledge of good and evil anywhere else.

Another evidence that man, the earth, and the world, are existing under and enduring the the displeasure of their Creator, arises from the fact that God himself, nor any of His holy angels, nor our redeemed friends in heaven, ever visit it. Some, doubtless, will not agree with this assertion, and affirm that God and the angels frequently visit our earth. This is not by any means to be admitted. The earth is so constructed, and is the subject of so much strife and contention, that it is not fitted or worthy of even a visit from the Almighty or His angels. An angel would scarcely be more inclined to leave the peace and bliss of heaven and to visit this world of strife, sin, and darkness, than a human being would visit the bottom of the ocean. The dangers of the one would scarcely be excelled by those of the other; yet either might be done, for with God all things are possible. By the aid of His omnipotent power any task may be accomplished; but this aid is never extended here on earth to any of His sinful creatures, except by spiritual manifestations. That we have the Spirit of God abiding in us is evident; without this we become a dead, rotten mass of ruin. This spiritual gift may be increased by works of godliness and prayer for the gift. It may

also be abused and lost for want of prayer and
righteousness, till the possessor is but little
above the brutes. I affirm that while God has
given us His Holy Spirit-and commandments,
neither He nor His angels ever visit this earth;
that there is no partiality in God, nor does He
suffer the same to exist among His angels or
saints; also, that His rewards and punishments are reserved for the resurrection from
the dead, and consequently there are no special providences on earth. It often happens
that such is seemingly the case, and that individuals are apparently saved from harm or
subjected to evil, and thus rewarded or punished by the special act of God; but all these
must be attributed to their proper causes, the
constant vicissitudes of this ever-changing
world. Man in his degraded state is continually on the alert for the help of his Creator;
he is conscious of his weakness and forlorn
condition, and seizes on any circumstance,
however trivial, to find evidences of God's favor, and sometimes of His displeasure; always
hoping for direct divine interposition and fa-

vor, yet conscious of the fact that God cannot and will not, in His impartiality, make these interpositions. Such would be unjust to the creatures of this world, and would be subjecting the world to two rewards or two punishments. This is likewise inconsistent with the teachings of Jesus Christ: he affirms, "For He maketh His sun to rise on the evil and on the good, and sendeth rain on the just and on the unjust." (See 5th chapter of St. Matthew.) This should be decisive of the matter, when it is so well established by observation.

Some will say that God made frequent visits to Moses in his time. Christ forbids that idea, so also does reason. "The Lord" spoken of by Moses in his writings was not the Creator of heaven and earth, but more probably an ecclesiastic of high pretensions. Many of the laws received by Moses from that source were of the most barbarous character, and were condemned by Christ in his teachings. Some of the deeds which he commanded Moses to perform were of the most heinous and diabolical description, such as are recorded, for instance, in 31st chapter of Numbers. Moses received and executed the law over the Israelites by his command, and it might seem that one of his objects in recording this, and many other acts equally condemned by our Saviour, was to expose the corruption and idolatry of this ruler, and to teach mankind that corruption and idolatry have always existed in this world, and that human nature has always been the same.

Some likewise contend that this earth of ours has frequently been visited by angels, and cite the visit of the angel to Balaam. This is a matter of mere history, and without doubt the ancients believed such to have been the fact. No doubt Saul believed the witch of Endor raised Samuel from the dead; but the apostles taught that Christ was the first to arise from the dead. So we must conclude that Saul was mistaken in the resurrection of Samuel; and it would be as reasonable to suppose that Balaam was also mistaken, and more especially when we know that no such things now occur.

Many other matters recorded in the Bible as special providences are merely typical of great events, and narrow risks, to which the ancient Israelites were exposed; and having the appearance of such, have been admitted into the Bible as part of their history. Such was the assertion of Joshua, that the sun and moon stood still while he fought a battle. Nothing of the like could have occurred, or even seemingly so. Joshua was elated with success, and no doubt wished to impress his countrymen with the importance of his victory, and, like some warriors of more modern ages, made a glowing report. There are many other matters contained in Bible history that have the appearance of impossibility without the direct interposition of God. They may be only emblematical of certain important truths or principles, and not realities; they were very likely clothed with surroundings which, if now known, would cause them to appear quite reasonable. These need not be stumbling-blocks or become rocks of offence to any, for they are only matters of history. Now it is and must be evident that

Moses never even saw God; yet the reader is apt to infer that Moses wished him to believe such was the fact. Moses frequently considered himself a type of the whole people of Israel from the beginning of earth to his day; and what his progenitors saw, he represents himself as seeing; and what they did, he represents himself as doing.

Without controversy, this earth has been visited by the powers of heaven since its curse, and it is likely that it was highly illuminated by the presence of some heavenly visitor, which was apparent to all the creatures of earth, and in this manner, or by a former millennium, the ancients derived their knowledge of heaven and God. Moses declared that he received the commandments of God from Mt. Sinai; that the Lord descended on it in fire, &c. Now Mount Sinai represents the splendid and elevated condition of earth at a former millennium, and the fire illustrates the brilliant illumination that prevailed when the angels preached the Gospel of Truth, and he impersonates the ancient Israelites who witnessed the display. This is the most plausible theory and construction that can be given to his narration of that event, and, as before observed, we are not to place an impossible construction, or even a contradictory one, on any teachings of the Bible, when, by a figurative construction, we can render it reasonable, consistent, and just.

These records of Bible history which seem contradictory, unreasonable, or impossible, might be well understood if we were but acquainted with their surroundings. As we are unacquainted with them in the present age, we cannot make the application of many of the figures contained in the Bible. If we could, I am fully persuaded that we could understand the nature of God, His angels, and of heaven, and the laws of their government. These have probably again and again been taught and explained by demonstration in millennial periods to mankind; but, owing to the backward state of science, our record is quite bare, century after century being contained in a few chapters.

It is evident that the ten commandments, or some of like nature, were given to mankind in the beginning, or that Adam brought them with him when he was driven out of the garden of Eden. "In the beginning was the Word." The Lord said unto Cain,. "If thou doest well, shalt thou not be accepted? if thou doest not well, sin lieth at the door." This is conclusive that mankind had the law at the beginning; by it Adam and all the earth have fallen.

This law is not confined to Christians, Jews, or refined nations; but the Gentiles, heathens, pagans, and all rational beings of earth, have it written in their hearts and instilled in their being. Wherever reason has a throne, there the law has a seat. It is true that this law becomes nearly effaced in individuals and nationalities, but cannot be entirely unseated from the human breast. The worst of savages, even cannibals, have the law engrafted in their natures, and are justly accountable for their deeds; though, to whom much is given, it is said, much will be required. Conscience exists

in all humanity, however depraved, and re-
proves guilt and crime in a heathen as well as
a christian. The same law governs all, and all
will be condemned or rewarded by it. Humanity is the same the world over, and the law is
the same not only on earth, but in heaven.

Some persons believe that Christ is God, and
that his visit to earth was a contradiction of the
statement that God and His angels do not visit
the earth. That Christ is the God of the Universe cannot be proved by the Scriptures, and
is condemned by reason. He never taught any
such doctrine. He taught that he was a son or
child of God, and that all other people were
who obeyed His laws. There is a vast difference between Christ and his Father, the living
supreme God. God is a Spirit, of whom we
cannot draw any perfect conceptions either of
His eternity, or power, or existence. We are
informed that His shape is similar to that of
man; also, that He has not flesh and blood as
we. Christ had, and visited this earth not as
God, but as man, having all the infirmities of
humanity upon him while sojourning on earth.

His visit here was his descent into Hades,
spoken of in the apocryphal writings. He
was, without controversy, one of the most illus-
trious visitors that has ever honored earth and
mankind. His mission on earth was prompted
by the most disinterested love and good-will
to mankind, and, unlike us, he came and endured the hardship, toil, strife, and death, of
this earth, not for any transgression of his
own, but that by his teachings and example
mankind might be blessed in eternity. He
died because of the sins of this world; arose,
and ascended to heaven, as all must do. He
was without sin either in heaven or earth, and
in this respect was divine. He was possessed
of powers far above human. He was not shorn
of some attributes of which human nature is;
or they were not crushed by his voluntary
visit to earth, as in our case, by the spiritual
fall from heaven to earth. He had powers of
which we are entirely shorn, or which have
been crushed by our fall from divine favor;
among these were spiritual sight, the power of
divining men's thoughts and hearts, and of do-

ing wonderful works. He was suffered to visit earth with these supernatural powers, because God had confidence that he would use or exert them for good, and not for evil. Hence he employed these supernatural powers only for good, and in no case for evil. The curse of the fig-tree was not an exception: he harmed that tree simply to confirm his teachings, and harmed it because it was inanimate or devoid of feeling; otherwise he might have made an example of a living human or other creature. In this respect Christ was divine. He never forfeited his estate in heaven by disobedience; and from his disinterested love to mankind (especially the poor and weak), from his total indifference to the wealth or honors of this world and the applause of men, and from the justness and purity of his teachings, and the holy and righteous example he set the people of earth, we are forced to acknowledge his divinity. This divinity enters into the existence of all of God's creatures. Life itself, as it exists in men and animals, is divine; but no creature of earth has ever possessed such divine powers as Jesus Christ. This divinity varies in life, and is in all probability proportioned to the magnitude or enormity of our past transgressions in the garden of Eden, or figurative heaven. This explains the difference in mankind and also animals. The transgressions of some were flagrant, and hence their degraded condition on earth; the transgressions of others were of less enormity, and hence their abundant intellect, wisdom, and better condition on earth.

Christ being without sin possessed superhuman powers, and enjoyed the confidence and favor of God. It was no part of his mission to change or alter the temporal condition of mankind or the laws of earth. The laws of heaven are immutable and firm; hence, when he assumed the frail flesh, body, and infirmities of man, he became, like us, subject to carnal death. This carnal death came not by Adam's transgression, but by our own, of similar nature to Adam's; hence we all must die, because we all have sinned. So immutable and firm are those laws, and so determined is

11

God's purpose that they shall not be relaxed, and they were not relaxed or dispensed with even in the case of an imploring and dutiful son; consequently, Christ himself suffered death rather than the laws of heaven should be violated.

But Christ's death and resurrection alone have not nor will not remove the curse of God from any one; neither will his example or teachings, unless we follow and obey them. Obedience to his teachings is the salvation he offered, and the means of our redemption in heaven; and the result of his teachings may be summed up or stated in a few words, and in language so plain that the wayfarer, though a fool, need not err therein. "Therefore all things whatsoever ye would that men should do to you, do ye even so them: for this is the law and the prophets." This he affirms to be the law and the doctrine of the prophets;— hence he did not change the law, for the law is truth, and existed from the foundation of the heavens and the earth. He taught no new doctrine, nor did he institute any meaningless ceremonies. He promulgated no metaphysical creeds. His religion was supreme love to God, and disinterested and unselfish love to our neighbor. It was the same that existed in the beginning, and is one and the same everlasting truth of the eternal God.

Christ was not God, but a teacher sent by God to resurrect truth on earth, which was almost crushed amidst the vanity, superstition, and idolatry of earth. For reproving these, he was unjustly condemned and suffered death, as we must. His offence was not blasphemy against God, as alleged, but merely exhibiting the folly and hypocrisy of the false teachings and idolatry of earth, as practised in metaphysical creeds and meaningless and superstitious ceremonies. He held forth the Golden Rule, above quoted, as the true religion of mankind. In no instance did he ever command a single ceremony to be performed by the inhabitants of earth; hence such only can exist by permission, and do not exist by command. From the manner in which he reprimanded the teachings and practices of the Jews, mankind must look with caution on the ceremonies of all our churches, even though they appear harmless, for they are too often calculated to lead astray from plain religious duties. They too often call mankind away from the strait gate and narrow way that leads to life everlasting, and make them the victims of idolatry and superstition. But more of this hereafter.

This earth, like man, possesses a two-fold nature. The first is for our instruction and reformation; the second is for our regeneration, and not ours only, but the regeneration of all its creatures into the realms of an endless, eternal, and sublime heaven. All of its creatures have fallen, and are degraded and far removed from God. This earth is merely a temporary sojourning-place for repentance toward God, whose divine laws all have violated. It, as combined with the powers of heaven, has power to resurrect and restore all to the realities of heaven, where all will be rewarded as their works shall deserve. The earth is specially designed to assist in the work of universal resurrection to heaven, as well as to teach and reform. All living creatures must prepare for the change from earth to heaven, for it is not distant. The Judge is even standing before our doors. The frost of the poles, and the heat, storms and poisonous winds from the tropics, are effectual destroyers of animal life. The impure air, water, and food, of which we are necessarily partakers, assist in our carnal death and spiritual resurrection.

We may view this earth from any standpoint, and we find that change, sin, decay, and death, are depicted on the whole. Why, reader, is this so? Why this continual change — this suffering — this misery? Why death? Why not a remedy except by pain, misery, and death? Why not a resurrection or transformation without it? We know that God in His omnipotence could relieve us, and why is this relief withheld? We are bound to admit one of two facts: first, that God is a petulant, inhumane Being; or, that we have flagrantly and wantonly violated His holy laws, established for the government of the eternal heavens, and therefore are now outcasts from the favors of heaven, and suffering punishment here on earth. This latter is the scriptural view, and is taught by reason, and must have the sanction of our best judgment. The whole face of the earth bears unmistakable marks of God's displeasure, and might aptly be called the wine-press of His wrath.

CHAPTER IV.

MAN.

HIS ORIGIN—THE GARDEN OF EDEN—THE FORBIDDEN FRUIT—HIS FALL—HIS EFFORTS TO PLEASE GOD—HIS PRAYERS -HIS RELIGION—HIS IDOLATRY—THE GOLDEN RULE THE TRUE GOSPEL—THE FOLLY OF PUBLIC PRAYER—OF CEREMONIES—THE PERVERSION OF GOSPEL TRUTH—FALSE TEACHERS—BIGOTS—OFFENCES AGAINST THE HOLY GHOST—HIS FAITH IN GOD—HIS DEATH AND BURIAL.

From the record in the first chapters of Genesis we are induced to believe that the human race once enjoyed a holy and exalted state in heaven. The language in which Moses wrote was barren and imperfect, and resort was of necessity had to the figures of speech. He gives an account of the creation of the heavens and the earth, and of man. The events of centuries are embraced in a few chapters.

That man and the heavens and the earth were made by an omnipotent God is a proposition that admits of no doubt, and is visible to all. As to the omnipotence of God, we see and know that it is beyond human comprehension. Moses informs us that the heavens and the earth were created by God "in the beginning"; that "the earth was without form" (that is, it was not the subject of the present existing state of affairs) "and void" (that is, the present race of men and administration of laws did not then exist), "and darkness was on the face of the deep"—this clause has reference to a time when the earth was not inhabited by any of God's creatures. The next passage says, "And the Spirit of God moved upon the face of the waters." The "Spirit of God" here alluded to clearly means the existence of heavenly beings as angels, because motion is ascribed to it, and this on the face of the waters. This motion on the face of the waters has a powerful meaning, and from it I derive my idea that water was in the beginning a solid, as glass, emeralds, pearls, &c. Light entered simultaneously with the moving of the Spirit of God; the heavens appeared, as also day and night. "And God called the firmament heaven." The land was divided from the seas; the vegetable kingdom was then formed, yielding seed and fruit after their kind. This, according to Moses, was all accomplished on the third day. What length of time was assigned to each day, or how time was reckoned, is not told, for the sun, moon and stars were not made till the fourth day. On the fifth day, God created the animal kingdom of the land, and of the sea, and of the air, "after their kind"; and on the sixth day, He created man. But, very properly, several questions here present themselves: Was the race of men here spoken of Adam and his posterity? Was the light spoken of in the first day that spoken of in the fourth day as emanating from the sun, moon and stars? Or.

was the earth once the habitation of angelic beings, existing in the favor of God and light of heaven, and moving upon the emerald-like waters? Moses says, "Then the heavens and the earth were finished, and all the host of them." What does the word *host* here mean, except an endless infinity? Again he says, after speaking of the sabbath of rest, "These are the generations of the heavens and of the earth when they were created, in the day that the Lord God made the earth and the heavens." Here one day is assigned to the creation. This generation of beings was entirely distinct from any now inhabiting this earth, and was not subject to the present evils of this earth. The earth was not then accursed, and there was no strife, pain, sin, or death. There were plants and herbs of the field before they grew; that is, the earth was picturesquely adorned and beautified so as to be pleasing in the sight of God and the holy creatures then inhabiting it.

Now in the 2d chapter, 6th verse, is another account of the creation of man. This was Ad-

am and Eve. But before they were created
sin and strife had entered the earth. It had
also rained upon the earth. This elastic atmosphere had enshrouded the earth, decom-
posing its former pure elements, reducing its
splendor, and destroying its original purity. .
What once was solid and neat as pearls, was,
by its constant action and strife, reduced to
dirt, filth, and fragments. It absorbed the at-
oms of water and again scattered them to earth
in the form of rain. At what precise time this
was done we cannot form any correct idea.
All that Moses could tell us, was, that it was
"in the beginning." It had rained, however,
and the dragon had been cast out together
with his angels (as narrated in the 12th chapter of Revelations), by Michael and his angels,
before Adam and Eve made their appearance
on earth.

Moses says Adam and Eve were placed in
the garden of Eden. Again the question arises,
where was or is the garden of Eden? Can it
be located on earth by any fair reasoning, or
description given by him? Most assuredly

not. They were placed in the garden at first accounts; they violated God's holy law there; they were also adjudged and condemned there, and afterwards driven out to till the ground from whence they were taken. Our first parents received their corporeal bodies from earth and their spiritual bodies from heaven. This is not the precise language of the Bible, but the inference is unmistakaby plain.

Let us now take a view of this garden as described by Moses. He represents it as containing many trees, among which was the tree of life and the tree of the knowledge of good and evil; and how many others we are not informed, but are left to conjecture that they were numerous. Of every tree of the garden they might freely eat, except the tree of the knowledge of good and evil, and the penalty of death was attached to the violation of this command. We cannot for a moment doubt that this description is a mere figure of speech, and that the tree and fruit are only typical of sin. The garden of Eden represents the heavens, or some portion of it other than this earth.

It seems that it might represent the limitless heavens, for they had access to every tree of the garden, and might enjoy the fruit of every tree except one, and that tree was this earth, which in that figure represents the tree of the knowledge of good and evil. The other trees represented the countless millions of heavenly bodies, as the planets, suns, and emerald-like spheres, which compose and adorn the heavens through the interminable confines of space. They were and are all good, and earth alone is vile, abounding in sin, vanity, strife, and idolatry. Hence our first parents were commanded not to partake of the fruit of earth, because, although pleasing to the sight, it was noxious and sinful. This command or admonition was disregarded by our first parents; they partook of the fruits of earth, or of the sin and vice of earth, and hence their shame, degradation and fall from heaven to earth. The Bible says they were driven out of the garden to till the ground from whence they were taken. Here was a removal from one place to another: these places are different—one is heaven, the other earth.

Christ, in speaking to Nicodemus, throws some light on this subject: he said, "No man hath ascended up to heaven, except he that came down from heaven." St. Peter, in his second general epistle, in speaking of false teachers, also elucidates this subject: he says, "For if God spared not the angels that sinned, but cast them down to hell, and delivered them into chains of darkness to be reserved unto judgment," &c. It cannot be doubted that all the souls of earth who have been regenerated by death and the resurrection have appeared before God by ascending to heaven. The Bible mentions many, and, God's laws being impartial and uniform, and His justice and mercy the same, it proves the resurrection and ascension of all. Therefore we are all fallen, and are outcasts of heaven, not for what Adam and Eve did, but for what we did ourselves; that is, partaking of the same fruit, the sin and vice, that Adam and Eve did.

Another evidence that the garden of Eden was and is heaven arises from the fact that it contained the "tree of life" and the "river," which we may very properly infer according to Revelations was the "river of life." Now, such river and tree do not exist on any portion of this earth, and never did; because Adam and Eve were cast or driven out of the garden lest they should eat of the tree of life and live forever. Some persist that because Moses mentions Ethiopia and Euphrates, the garden was located on earth; but geographers confess they cannot so locate it. There is no locality on earth that will suit the description; travellers and explorers have found no such tree as the tree of life, nor any such river or water as the fountain of life. Such tree and river only exist in the blissful realms of heaven, the true Eden. Adam and Eve there enjoyed heaven's eternal joys, but in an evil hour transgressed the commands of God and were banished to earth. Time with them was not precious as on earth; space or distance was of but little importance to them; they went forth to any portion of the garden or distant heavens, as developed in stars, planets, suns, &c., at will, and with the rapidity of thought. There was

no impure, boisterous atmosphere, or unfavor-
able wind, to arrest their passage or impede
their flight; there was no weariness, no thirst,
no hunger, nor sorrow, nor tears, nor pain, nor
death, in their heavenly abode. They were
not then the subjects of disordered flesh, impure blood, aching bones, nor vicious appe-
tites, and, if they had resisted temptation and
sin, might have enjoyed the favor of the living
God through all eternity. The whole range of
heaven was theirs and the enjoyments thereof
all granted them, except the fruits of earth,
which are sin, folly, strife and idolatry: these
were denied them for their own benefit. Their
knowledge of good was derived from heaven;
their knowledge of evil could be acquired only
on earth, as it nowhere else exists.

After Adam partook of the forbidden fruit,
(i. e. the crimes, vanities and follies of earth,)
he was sent forth, or driven out, from this heavenly garden to till the ground from whence he
was taken. So complete and effectual was his
fall, that " cherubim were placed at the east of
of the garden of Eden, and a flaming sword

which turned every way, to keep the way of the tree of life." This "flaming sword" represents death, and the "cherubim" represent the angels of the resurrection, and restoration of Adam and his posterity to heaven. The serpent represents the carnality of earth.

Adam's violation was positive, so the judgment of God was swift, and his punishment commensurate with his guilt; and though his chastisement was severe, yet how comparatively short with the duration of eternity! Although doomed to a world of sin and darkness, pain and death, his sentence was but as for a moment. Guardian angels were placed at the gates, and his Creator stood at the door to welcome his return and conduct him back to heaven. Without doubt Adam's atonement was complete for his own transgression, and he is now enjoying the bliss of heaven.

Just in like manner as Adam fell, so all the earth have fallen; and in like manner as he made atonement, all the earth must. When Adam was driven to the earth, he found himself in a world of sin, misery, and death. He needed no inspiration to inform him of his loss. Misery, toil, suffering, pain, sorrow, and death, everywhere confronted him; the recollection of heaven' and his present degradation bore heavily upon him, and his loss was manifest. So with all that enter the limits of this earth. We enter in pain and misery, live in pain and misery, and depart in the same manner. Our earthly abode is one of change, and from the turmoil and strife of earth all creatures, whether rational or irrational, must soon depart. The earth is one great panorama of sin, strife, and death. We enjoy but few comforts on it. We enter it in helpless infancy, and only by the aid of kind parents or friends could survive for a day, or ever attain manhood. As we advance in life, the troublesome character of earth becomes more and more apparent to us, till at length the solemn idea that we are in a world of toil, sin, disease, and death, becomes patent and is firmly impressed on our minds. The changes of earth are constantly transpiring—misery still enduring, and death still completing its work of destruction.

In the midst of earth's changes and convulsions, the most untutored mind discovers that we cannot exist without some protection from the storms of earth; so mankind, even in early youth, recognize the fact that labor is necessary to procure food, raiment, and shelter. So we intrench ourselves as best we can against the seasons and changes; but as we build, time destroys. Labor and industry relieve only temporarily, and it is only by continued toil and exertion that mankind can enjoy protection from the raging elements. The soil yields thistles and thorns spontaneously, and but few fruits and cereals without labor. It abounds in stones, dirt, &c.; but food, raiment and shelter must be obtained by the sweat of our brows. To this end mankind engage in active labor to retrieve their ruined condition. They may, and in fact do, ameliorate their hard fate by labor and science; but the curse under which they groan can only be removed by an entire change in the organic laws of earth. Strife must be banished from earth, otherwise the creatures thereof must forever be its victims. As fast as we build, the elements destroy; as fast as food and raiment are produced, they are consumed and worn out, or time destroys. All the productions and creatures of earth must soon pass away; so with the pleasures and comforts of man, they are but transient in their nature, and soon disappear. As season succeeds season, so one generation succeeds another; and there is no certainty in life. Death is certain, and will forever be so while strife abounds on earth.

In this world scarcely anything is pure except the holy Spirit of God that is implanted in us all, and which gives us life and hope, and also the light we enjoy directly from heaven. These two, at least, are pure and divine, and the one is just as indestructible as the other, as impartial and just as the other, when free.

Man, in order to live and avoid death, has resorted to every possible experiment and practice; death to him has untold terrors, and life has anxieties the most intense. He has scaled and undermined mountains, traversed the seas, and perambulated every portion of earth accessible to him, in search of things that would better his condition, or alleviate, if but for a moment, his sufferings; and if, perchance, he might discover the tree of life, or fountain of living water. It is not to be denied that he improves his condition by commerce; but the tree of life, or fountain of living water, does not exist on earth; hence his searches in that behalf have and will prove vain.

In his misery and degradation he very naturally turns his mind and thoughts to God, and seeks relief by prayer. He sees that he is doomed to a world of strife and sin, and that he is overwhelmed by death, and consigned to oblivion and the grave. He has used every earthly exertion within human power to avoid his fate, and entreats his Creator for mercy and life. This mercy has not been, and, we may confidently affirm, never will be, granted. God's laws are as immutable to man as to earth. His life-blood is demanded as an atonement for his transgressions, and death must ensue before he can enjoy the favor of heaven. Man has in all ages been a creature of prayer. He has instituted ceremonies, made sacrifices, sung pæans of praise, to endeavor to reinstate himself in the divine favor, and to gain relief from the strife, sin, and death, enshrouding earth. His ceremonies, his sacrifices, his songs of praise, have all proved unavailing. Many of them are of the most foolish and absurd description, as if to appease His wrath with folly, —if, perchance, He might be a whimsical God. No effort, creed, ceremony, or incantation, has been left untried. Sin, strife, and death, still abound; for God is unchangeable, and not to be entreated for temporal blessings, and will not heed prayer for such.

It is a matter of astonishment as well as curiosity to read of the ceremonies and sacrifices performed by mankind to gain favor with God. These ceremonies and sacrifices are coëval with their history, while most all of them are of the most meaningless description. When the transgressor's own blood was required by an omnipotent God, he endeavored to appease his Creator with that of bulls, goats, and rams. In sacrificing these on an altar which he first dedicated to God by numerous ceremonies, he performed divers incantations and prayed divers prayers; but God's judgment remained and still remains firm; His laws are the same, and must remain the same.   There is no relief on earth, but relief comes in death to all who obey God's word. Death—this carnal body of ours being left destitute of the Spirit of God—is the new birth and remedy for man's ills. No entreaties to God have or will ever enable a single mortal to escape this. Even our Saviour was subjected to it, and how futile it is for mortals to pray for relief from death, or for worldly joys or benefits.

Prayers for heavenly favors are appropriate, but those prompted by earthly gains are unholy. Most of the prayers made by humanity are for temporal advantages, and wicked in their nature, and should not nor cannot be granted by an impartial God. The apostle St. James says, "Ye ask, and receive not, because ye ask amiss, that ye may consume it upon your lusts." How absurd it is for sensible and reasonable beings to implore God to interpose His partiality in their behalf! God cannot be tempted by prayer, or any other means, to partiality or favoritism; yet how much of the religion of the present day is founded on that assumption. Men are taught to pray for God's aid, and without doubt do pray for it, in all their business relations of life, however reprehensible or wicked their pursuits may be. The evil-disposed man, if possible, would strengthen his nerves and increase his energies by prayer, even while engaged in the most abominable work, such as robbing his fellow-man and destroying his life.

What logic is there in prayer for success in earthly pursuits? If the merchant loads his ship with food and clothing, and dispatches her and cargo to a distant port, why should he seek the interposition of God in his favor, and to crown the enterprise with success? Does he not know that, in order to prove a grand success, as he probably prays for, the people of the foreign port must be in sore need of food and raiment? What right has he to expect God to afflict those people with hunger and nakedness that he may extort a few corruptible dollars from them? What would you think of your druggist, if he should procure an immense stock of drugs, and then pray publicly to Almighty God for quick sales and large profits? Such prayers are but profanity. As well might the manufacturer of arms and munitions of war implore God for a quick and ready sale for his implements of death—the plain meaning of which would be for war and bloodshed. All such prayers are merely taking the name of the Lord in vain, and are prompted by Satan. Most of the prayers of this world are of just such a nature, being prompted by covetousness and greed—some through the most damnable desires that fallen humanity can conceive. No wonder God does not heed them, for they are most abominable in His sight.

There are prayers, however, which are not only proper, but a duty that every one owes to God; such, for instance, as the Lord's prayer, contained in a few verses of the New Testament. That is highly commendable, but, in this age of prayers, has, like nearly all else of true religion, become nearly obsolete, and its place supplied by more fashionable and glowing ones. How repulsive to all religious sentiment it is to hear a minister, after asking a worshiping assembly to kneel in prayer, to commence lecturing the Almighty for His short-comings and remissness of duty in not showing His partiality in a more conspicuous manner among the inhabitants of earth, and especially to his particular church; and then commence petitioning for ideal blessings, and, as he waxes warm, or becomes impassionate, to pray for fire or some abomination or evil to befall the earth from heaven. If these ministers, whom the world calls gifted in prayer, could have their impious petitions granted, the world could not endure. Such is human nature. We are continually beseeching God to relieve us from our infirmities, and also imploring Him to excuse us for not doing the identical thing that he requires us to do, viz., to obey the golden rule as given by Jesus Christ in the seventh chapter of St. Matthew's Gospel: "Therefore all things whatsoever ye would that men should do to you, do ye even so to them: for [says Christ] this is the law and the prophets."

God's language to Cain, in the beginning, was, "If thou doest well, shalt thou not be accepted? and if thou doest not well, sin lieth at the door." Solomon said, "Let us hear the conclusion of the whole matter: Fear God and keep His commandments; for this is the whole duty of man. For God shall bring every work into judgment, with every secret thing, whether it be good, or whether it be evil." (Eccles. xii. 13, 14.) Here is ample proof that religion is and always was the same: "In the beginning was the Word." Religion is simple in its nature and teachings; it consists of no metaphysical creeds, meaningless ceremonies, or vain prayers; but is supreme love and adoration to God, and unselfish love, justice, and mercy, to our neighbor. Its whole essence is embraced in the golden rule, which embodies all the essentials of religion. All the teachings of Moses and the prophets, and of Christ and his apostles, were details or amplifications of the golden rule. All ceremonies are mere shadows or illustrations of religion, and are of no value or importance only as a means of setting forth the truth of the Gospel. The *truth* is the Gospel and religion; and whatever is not truth, is not Gospel or religion.

Christ said his yoke was easy and his burden light. He taught no ceremonies. His religion was the golden rule, and that our reward would be according to our works. His doctrines and teachings have to some extent been discarded by his own followers and teachers, and the worst of heresies substituted; one of which is, that an individual may violate and trample his religion under his feet nearly all his life and then gain the chief favors in heaven by prayer, and performing certain ceremonies, and making certain confessions. This golden rule is a matter that requires mankind to perform various duties, all of which are just, sensible, and merciful; and mankind must be on

their guard if they would not come short of its
requirements and the glory of God.   Now this
glory we all desire, but it does not suit us to
live up to the golden rule ; hence we have instituted certain rites and ceremonies which all
rational intelligent persons know are not religion, and were not instituted to promote religion, but just the reverse, that is, to dispense
with the duties of religion.

This love to our neighbor required by religion is at times quite exacting ; it requires us
sometimes to part with a portion of our money, our food, our raiment ; at other times it requires our personal labor. It requires, indeed,
our constant watch, and we are to be ready at
all times to perform its exigencies.   Hence we
have resorted to means to dispense, if possible,
with the exactions of the religion of the golden
rule. Prayer is made the chief panacea or king
cure-all for all our sins and short-comings, and,
though the subject is ever so vile, and has led
a life ever so wicked and depraved, we are told
by the preachers that prayer is the remedy.
So far as it can be, they have reduced it to a

science, and the wicked transgressor is taught to use it without stint—to pray earnestly and fervently, and his sins will be wiped or blotted out and remembered no more; and especially so, if he will confess, recite an absurd creed, and submit to an ablution, immersion, pouring, or sprinkling, called baptism.

Christ taught no such doctrine, but precisely the reverse. He first taught the golden rule, and also restitution when possible. In his sermon on the mount he said, " Therefore, if thou bring thy gift to the altar, and there rememberest that thy brother hath aught against thee, leave there thy gift before the altar, and go thy way; first be reconciled to thy brother, and then come and offer thy gift. Agree with thine adversary quickly, whiles thou art in the way with him," &c. (Matt. v. 25-27.) Here he preached a plain, honest duty that was to be performed; that is, that we must do justice to our brother; and not only our brother, but to our adversary. How could he truthfully preach other doctrine, or how could he expect an impartial and just God to extend His for-

giveness, when it would be the means of pro-
moting injustice and wrong? God will never
pardon an individual when wrong and sin
would thereby triumph. Hence there are certain offences that He will not pardon, such as
offences committed by one brother or neighbor
against another. We each and all have his
Holy Spirit dwelling in us, giving us life and
existence, and these offences against each other
are, properly speaking, offences against the
Holy Ghost, for which there is no forgiveness
in heaven. "Know ye not that ye are the tem-
ples of God, and that the Spirit of God dwell-
eth in you." (1 Cor. iii. 16.) Upon restitution,
or proper efforts at restitution, and often by
even contrite confession of the transgressing
brother or neighbor, we must forgive, or the
sin lieth at our door.

This principle of religion called forgiveness
is the most important and all-powerful means
of a glorious salvation known to the people of
earth. Christ teaches us to pray for forgiveness as we forgive others. This is one of the
most serious and solemn lessons inculcated in

all his teachings, that when, humbled in prayer, beseeching the favors and mercies of heaven, we are not to ask or expect any which we would deny to others. How all-important, then, does this question become! How cautious should mankind be lest they treasure up in their hearts relentlessness and revenge even with their enemies! This important matter is impressed on our minds by Christ in the parable of the cruel and wicked servant and creditor. See the 18th chapter of Matthew—read it, by all means—and see also the 6th chapter of Matthew, which teaches that we will be forgiven as we forgive one another. God, being just and benevolent, will be found more lenient in judgment than even a father to his own son; hence if we forgive each other, so will He forgive us. By the christian and liberal exercise of this grace, many of us poor mortals will undoubtedly find ourselves astonished in the resurrection and judgment at the beneficent reward bestowed upon us. Instead of finding our sins and faults all charged against us by our neighbors and meeting deserved punishment, we will probably not find a vestige of them, because forgiven both by our neighbors and God himself.

Here let me observe, mankind are much better than they generally have credit for, and as a rule do not generally treasure up each other's wrongs, and for this reason alone cannot be condemned in the judgment. Christ taught, "If ye then, being evil, know how to give good gifts unto your children, how much more shall your Father which is heaven give good things to them that ask him?" Man is not, nor never was, deficient in prayer: he is always imploring the divine aid both in temporal and heavenly matters. The fault lies with man that he asks and receives not. He asks amiss—he asks for blessings that God cannot righteously grant; but all that He can so grant, will not be withheld in the judgment to come.

Man's praying disposition also proves him to be a much better being than he is accredited for. He has unbounded confidence in God's mercy and goodness, and no want of faith. He prays, and gains no advantage or favor of a temporal nature; but nothing baffled, or none the less confident, he offers prayer after prayer. If faith will save man, then his salvation is a matter of certainty; and so with prayer. But the truth is, neither will suffice without works. This golden rule, laid down and written in man's heart from the foundation of the world, must be observed and obeyed. Prayer cannot dispense with it, neither can faith or the performance of religious rites. "By their fruits ye shall know them." Prayer has no application on earth: the good suffer with the evil, and the righteous with the wicked. The prayer of neither, even for bread, will not be answered, because God's rewards are not in this world. The righteous often suffer for bread while the wicked oppressor riots in wealth and luxury. If God's interposition were made at all, He would interpose in favor of the righteous, weak, and suffering. The wicked triumph as often as the righteous in this world. Justice often gives place to injustice, and the strong wrongfully oppress and

13

even rob and murder the weak. This, however, by no means proves that God does not exist, or that He is indifferent to justice and righteousness, but simply that His judgment is reserved for the resurrection.

The affairs of men and this world are governed by laws the most impartial and the most just, and God refuses to interfere in any manner with the affairs of earth from the fact that man is a transgressor of His just laws, and has voluntarily relinquished and forfeited his claims to the divine favor. So long as he is a sojourner in the flesh and the world he is delivered over to evil, and for the time being must endure the sins and evils of earth. Hence we cannot find any earthly favor with God. We may find spiritual favor, but not carnal favor. This proves that the earth and man are under God's displeasure. Man has endeavored by every imaginable means to please God, but all to no avail. We cannot please Him in the flesh, but must endure carnal death and be resurrected in heaven, which is simply the new birth spoken of by our Saviour.

I have already affirmed that Christ taught no metaphysical creeds or meaningless ceremonies. Nicodemus came to Jesus by night, and it seems was inquiring the way of salvation. Christ gave him a brief lecture and dismissed him without requiring him to make a single confession or perform a single ceremony. The presumption is that he was a good ruler and just man, for he was not commanded to do anything, or even pray. He was astonished at the simplicity of Christ's doctrine, and seems to have been expecting to receive some mysterious creed, or commanded to perform some imposing ceremony. Such was not the fact, for he was told that he must be born again—of water and of the Spirit—before he could enter the kingdom of heaven. The water here means the natural death of the body, and the resurrection is the new birth. If otherwise, Nicodemus was left without advice, for he was not commanded to do a single thing. (See 3d chapter of St. John's Gospel.)

The next instance was a ruler, who inquired the way of salvation. Jesus answered him:

"Thou knowest the commandments, Do not commit adultery, Do not kill, Do not steal, Do not bear false witness," &c. And he said, "All these have I kept from my youth up." Now just here we may very properly infer from the sequel that this ruler was guilty of falsehood; but which could not be concealed from Jesus, as he had a power not possessed by us, that of divining men's thoughts. This ruler was very rich, and without doubt had not obtained his wealth legitimately, or by honest trade, or by labor and frugality. In other words, he was an usurer, and oppressor of the poor: hence, he was commanded to sell his property and distribute to the poor (whom he had very probably oppressed and wronged), and also follow him; that is, for the future to obey the golden rule. He gave him no creed to ponder over, nor did he command him to perform a single rite, but required him to do a substantial act of justice—that is, make restitution. (See 18th chapter of St. Luke.)

The third instance was a certain lawyer, who stood up and tempted him, saying, "Master, what shall I do to inherit eternal life? He said unto him, What is written in the law? how readest thou? And he answering said, Thou shalt love the Lord thy God with all thy heart, and with all thy soul, and with all thy strength, and with all thy mind; and thy neighbor as thyself. And he said unto him, Thou hast answered right: this do, and thou shalt live." This is recorded in the 10th chapter of St. Luke's Gospel.

St. Mark (chapter 12) records a conversation similar to the above between Christ and one of the scribes: "And when Jesus saw that he answered discreetly, he said unto him, Thou art not far from the kingdom of God."

These instances, combined with his sermon on the mount, most undoubtedly include the whole system of the Christian religion; otherwise the system is defective and his teachings imperfect. And if his system of religion was perfected by him, the religious world must look elsewhere for their ordinances and ceremonies, for he neither taught nor commanded the observance of any.

St. John informs us that Christ "baptized not." John did baptize with water, but said, "One cometh after me," meaning Christ; "he shall baptize you with the Holy Ghost and with fire. (See 3d chapter of St. Luke.) The baptism of John and Christ was different. John baptized with water, while Christ's baptism was with spiritual teaching and Gospel truth; hence John likens it to fire. It is quite evident from the Scriptures that some of the apostles and disciples followed up John's baptism, and some we learn even baptized unto John, or in honor of John, as may be inferred. Paul "thanked God" that he baptized only a few, and named them, and said he was sent by Christ "not to baptize, but to preach the Gospel." See 1st chapter I. Corinthians; see also the 10th chapter, where he taught that "all our fathers were under the cloud, and all passed through the sea; and were all baptized unto Moses in the cloud and in the sea."

Now we have baptism by sprinkling, by pouring, by immersing; baptism unto Moses, unto John, unto Christ, and did have, without doubt, unto others. We have it in and with the water, in the sea, and in the cloud; we have it with the Holy Ghost, and, to cap the climax, with that dreadful thing, fire. We have also misery and praying the world over. The chief priests, the scribes and elders asked Christ a question : " By what authority doest thou these things ?" Before consenting to reply thereto, Christ asked them one question : "The baptism of John, was it from heaven or men ? Answer me." (See 11th chapter of St. Mark.) Here he speaks of baptism as a thing of the past. Also in the 10th chapter he spake of a baptism that he was baptized with, meaning his crucifixion and death, with which all shall be baptized. Paul, perceiving the Gospel truth of Christ, taught that all the law was fulfilled in one word, even in this, "Thou shalt love thy neighbor as thyself," and that circumcision shall profit nothing, for by the works of the law shall no flesh be justified. (See first chapters of epistle to Galatians.) Justification by ceremonies is impossible, and the only possible excuse that christians can adduce for ceremonious worship is for illustration of heavenly things by them.

John's baptism is a mystery, and the reasons calling for its adoption are not now apparent; yet he undoubtedly had good reasons for it at the time. Let this matter be as it may, Christ did not practise it, and the same might be said of some of the apostles; and if it is a matter of such serious importance to mankind as some believe, then Christ is at fault in not explaining more definitely its virtue and importance. This we are not to presume, nor impute fault to Christ; better by far surrender the rite. In all his teachings we find the utmost good sense and reasoning, as well as truth and justice; but this water baptism is devoid of reason and common sense, and was probably performed in honor and remembrance of John's labors, and the unjust and cruel manner in which he lost his life. Religion is addressed to rational beings, and is itself rational as well as truth; and when religion is void of reason, we may well affirm that it is only idolatry. I call idolatry the

profession of any religious creed, or the performance of any religious ceremony or act,
that is devoid of reason and common sense. I
call a ceremony, or rite, the performance of a
religious act that is esteemed by the actor to
be really essential to his salvation. Hence
the Lord's supper is not a ceremony, but a
commemorative service and an emblem of charity; and is not to be condemned, but highly
esteemed.

It may be truthfully asserted that Christ did
not in any instance teach any rite or ceremony. The institution of the Holy Sacrament is
not an exception. It was instituted that his
example and teachings might be perpetuated
in the memory of the world, and also to inculcate lessons of charity. The bread he administered to his disciples is emblematical of that
charity which all true christians must administer to the suffering poor; and the wine is
emblematical of his spiritual teachings, which
are to be administered to the young and ignorant—which is his baptism. This is to be done
in remembrance of him; not that he was de-

sirous of the applause of men, or the honor or riches of this world, but that his example and teachings might be perpetuated, and his charity (taught thereby) practised, and the world benfitted both temporally and eternally. Here we have the utmost good sense as well as reason, and consequently the performance of this command is a christian duty, being a method of inculcating and perpetuating truth, and is not idolatry. This is not even a necessary part of religion, but a means of evidencing love for Christ and his Gospel.

In this view of the matter, we clearly see the reason why St. Paul cautioned the Corinthians to examine themselves before partaking of the supper. The supper is an emblem of charity; and if any, for instance, who are able to work, shall go about seeking charities and begging alms unworthily, then they are to be damned. This charity is the Lord's body, and those that partake unworthily will suffer for it. The wine is emblematical of his holy truth and justice, and the damnation is directed against hypocrites and disbelievers, who are found in the church for temporal and sinister advantages. In this view, any charitable man or woman that admires Christ's Gospel may very properly partake of the supper or sacrament. It is a commemorative act, and was designed to inculcate lessons of love, charity, and truth; and also to teach humility, and the great fact that we do not live altogether for ourselves, but in part for God and our neighbor, be that neighbor whoever it may. We must bear each other's burdens occasionally. We must administer charity even if impostors and hypocrites and vagabonds occasionally become partakers. God will reward them. Who would burn a barn of grain to destroy a few rats and mice? Who would refuse to harvest a field of wheat because there were a few tares in it? If hypocrites deceive us, they cannot deceive God; so let us be charitable.

The healing of the blind man, recorded in the 9th chapter of St. John's Gospel, is no evidence that ceremonies are proper. It is true that Christ spat on the ground, and made clay of the spittle, and anointed the eyes of the blind man, and commanded him to wash in the pool of Siloam, and that he washed and came seeing; yet we are not at liberty to suppose that Christ perfected this cure by means of sorcery, or that the clay, spittle or washing was the cause of the blind man's seeing, or had any agency in the cure; but we must refer the cure to Christ's divinity, and not to legerdemain. Some, however, would have Christ appear as a mere magician or sorcerer, in order to justify senseless doctrines, or meaningless ceremonies. Christ was not a dealer in hocus pocus, nor a professor of legerdemain, but a teacher of the rational and everlasting truths of God. He resorted to no magic ceremony in effecting any of his work, nor in teaching any of his truths. The more rational interpretation of the blind man's cure is, that, as he was blind from his birth, his eyes were in a condition to need washing; and as the man was helpless and blameless, and washing necessary, Christ took this mode to secure a proper ablution rather than create unpleasant feelings in a helpless man. Christ was really a polite, humane man, if it is proper to call him a man. His cure of the deaf man, recorded in the 7th chapter of St. Mark's Gospel, was not effected by conjury. Christ put his fingers into his ears, and he spit and touched his tongue, and looking up to heaven sighed and said, " Be opened." Now here is a semblance of conjury, but on examination we find it quite different. This man was deaf, that is, he was shorn of one sense which nearly all possess; he had no idea of a thing like sound, nor was he acquainted with the power of speech. As he could neither hear nor talk, he was ignorant of many of his surroundings. Other men had ears, and so he knew he had; as others had mouths and tongues, he knew he had, and could move the same as they. Still he was unconscious of sound or speech; he knew not the use of his ears, or what his tongue was made for, except for the purposes he used them, that is, eating, drinking, spitting, tasting, &c. He was unconscious of Christ's powers, and was without faith in him, for Christ was in appearance as the rest of mankind. So

Christ was to awaken in this man a sense of his defects—that is, that there was the sense of hearing and power of speech, and also faith in him, and for this purpose he employed these simple means. All mankind are defective in certain senses and powers, of which we even can form no more conception than the deaf man; and if these senses or powers were restored, mankind would be perfect as the angels. One of these, of which we are shorn, is spiritual sight.

It is not my design in this work to justify or condemn any man's religion, or the religious creeds or ceremonies of any particular denomination, but simply to prove that religion is truth, and that truth is founded on reason and justice; but the teachings of metaphysical creeds and meaningless ceremonies are to be condemned where they mislead or deceive. At present, when a young man is educated for the ministry, the important truths embraced in the golden rule, or true Gospel, is a matter of minor importance. He is educated not to teach and inculcate the love, justice, charity, mercy, and humility, that this Gospel exacts, but too often to defend a meaningless batch of creeds and ceremonies. To this end he searches the Bible for isolated passages bearing on the subject, or aiding him in his defence; he reads learned commentators (learned in such sectarian dogmas); and finally, if he is able to make a good defence of the religious creeds or rites of his particulaar church, he is accounted worthy for the ministry—when the all-patent truth is, he is scarcely better qualified for a preacher than he is for a juggler. His study has not been how to inculcate and enforce the Gospel precepts, but to show how their force may be avoided.

This doctrine of faith without works, to say the least of it, is one of the most dangerous ever preached to an inquiring world. The idea that a person can neglect and even disdain the love, justice and mercy contained in the golden rule, and then in the eleventh hour, if you please, give a reward equal to those who have obeyed it through life, is questionable, if not absurd and impossible. The parable of the laborers in the vineyard, at first view, would seem to warrant this, but on closer inspection it does not. The laborers that came in at the eleventh hour received full pay ; not, however, for idleness or vice, but because they were ready and in search of employment. These men would have willingly worked all day, but no employment was offered. And it often happens the same in life; men do not work because necessity nor charity does not require it. If the naked are clothed, the hungry fed, the young and ignorant taught, and the stranger entertained, &c., we are left without christian works, and consequently must of necessity wait for employment; but if we hope to receive full reward we must be like the laborers, on the watch; and not only on the watch, but must work when called. God, in His abundance, will then reward all alike, for all have performed their duty.

So also with the parable of the prodigal son. He became tired of serving his father, demanded his portion, went into a far country, and there wasted his substance in riotous living;

but after he had expended all, he returned to his father, and was joyfully welcomed. This parable is only typical of the idolater; the phrase "devouring thy living with harlots" is typical of idolatrous worship; "living" represents truth, which was sacrificed for idolatry. The offence of this prodigal was one directly against God, and one that He could righteously pardon, and consequently did so; but if the offence had been of a different nature, and directed against the children of God or Holy Ghost—that is, if the prodigal had returned stained with covetousness, oppression, theft, and the blood of his fellow-men—his reception would have been different. He was addicted to idolatry, and had become convinced of the error of its teachings and practices, and was fully impressed with its emptiness; hence he repented or turned away from it, and sought the truth, the living of his father. He approached his father with the truth, and was joyfully received. Idolatry may or may not be sin; but so far as it misleads, it is to be condemned.

14

The case of the thief on the cross is often cited for the eleventh hour doctrine. The spiritual condition of one of those thieves who were crucified with Christ was excellent. He was, or had been, a violator of God's law; he confessed it and was expiating his guilt on the cross, and that willingly. Suppose the persons from whom he had stolen were there present observing his crucifixion, would they not have forgiven him, without restitution, on his confession and severe atonement then being inflicted on him? Had they not already done so? If not, they should have done so, for he was making all the recompense and atonement that mortal could do, and that willingly and honestly ; hence he was a proper case for pardon. Here it may be observed, that if an individual is forced by the temporal law to make restitution or atonement for transgression, and the atonement and restitution is full, ample, and just, then God will forgive whenever the individual confesses its justice and asks forgiveness; but it is futile to ask if we have not performed our duty to the injured party. We must make recompense, and then confess our faults, first to the injured party, then to God; and never to preachers, unless for advice—unless, perchance, we have injured the preacher.

Christ gives us a lesson in the parable of the good shepherd, in the 10th chapter of St. John's Gospel, concerning the attempt to gain admission to heaven except by the Gospel truths. He was addressing the Pharisees, a sect of Jews quite fond of ceremonies, traditions of the elders, and long prayers. He said, "He that entereth not by the door into the sheepfold, but climbeth up some other way, the same is a thief and robber." This scathing rebuke to the ceremonies, hypocrisies, and long prayers of the Jews, was not understood by them till an exposition of the same was made by him; but after they understood its meaning, they accused him of having a devil and of being mad, so offensive was the truth to them.

The Bible is full of evidence that mankind will and must be judged by their works. Religion and faith in God are proved by works.

No man can believe that God exists in omnipotent power, and that He reigns in a heaven of
unbounded glory, and that He will resurrect
him after death, and reward him through all
eternity according to his works on earth, without making some efforts to gain that reward.
A man cannot believe without working. Hence
we see some men that the world calls wicked,
or "hard cases," foremost in works of real
charity; even poor men, who have no money
or property to bestow, are often found laboring much of their time to render comfortable
others less fortunate; who sometimes take
large tasks upon themselves for the benefit of
others, well knowing that they will receive no
pay in this world. Now, inquire into this
matter, and you will find that the gospel of
the golden rule is forcing them to this conduct; it is impleading in their hearts to extend
mercy and help to others, as they would like
if conditions were changed. This golden rule
and sermon on the mount is written in the
hearts of all, Christian, Pagan, heathen, civilized, and barbarous. It makes us a law unto

ourselves, and is the Gospel of Christ and religion of God. Men should not be taught for an instant to disregard it, and, in case they transgress it, no hope of pardon should be held out, except by restitution or confession to the injured party, and pardon by him if restitution cannot be made; after which he may pray God for His forgivness, and for fortitude to resist wrong and temptation in the future.

How much better for society, and how much safer, is the performance of the requirements of the golden rule! It is peace, happiness, and power, to nationalities. Every one, in fact, loves the justice, mercy, and benefits flowing from the exercise of this rule, however little they may be inclined to live up to it. Hence, nations who obey its teachings and observe it most closely, always thrive best, and their subjects are happier and more prosperous than any on earth. The rule is so plain that all can comprehend it, having nothing mysterious about it. Its strict observance begets a high degree of civilization and national prosperity. Mankind can immeasurably improve their earthly welfare by it, and in fact do so, and they should all observe it for this reason, even if there was no prize in eternity. But Christ promised blessings on earth, and life eternal in heaven, to all who obey it. Then it behooves us all to engage in works of charity and forgiveness, the most excellent graces of earth, compared to which all others, aside from love, are as sounding brass and tinkling cymbals.

But how is it with the religion of creeds, ceremonies, penances, &c.? People listen to their articles of faith; they say they repent, they confess, and submit to their creeds and ordinances. They return home, and find themselves the same corrupt, degraded beings; they have the same hardships, toils, temptations, sins, and death, to encounter as before; and, besides, have numerous confessions (some of which are false, and required to be public) to make and duties to perform not otherwise required. As soon as their religious excitement vanishes, a great many become disgusted at the useless requirements of the church, and unjust restraints imposed upon them, and finally abandon the church; or, as St. Peter more forcibly declares, "But it is happened unto them according to the true proverb: The dog is returned to his own vomit again, and the sow that was washed to her wallowing in the mire." St. Peter says, "It had been better for them not to have known the way of righteousness"; but it is to be hoped that he would allow a difference between righteousness and unreasonable creeds and burdensome ceremonies. Others, by the power of this Gospel truth, become truly converted; and others, having always been the best of Christians, and believing duty to call them into church organizations, endure these creeds, make the confessions, and perform the useless ceremonies of the church, all their lives. Yes, they have these burdens to carry all their lives, or be disgracefully ejected from the church.

But some will say, how shall men worship? Worship God in spirit, truth, and reason; perform the duties required by the golden rule, from the cradle to the grave; let what may happen, cling to truth and right; honor God by building churches, preaching the truth in them, and by singing and praying appropriate prayers; have rules of decorum and strict behavior during worship, and also such just and reasonable rules as the welfare of the church requires. But lay aside creeds and ceremonies; these caused dissensions among Christ's chosen apostles. When they met at Jerusalem (see Acts xv.) to consider of these dissensions concerning circumcision, how effectually was it disposed of. It was declared not important; and no other ceremony was ever discussed among the apostles, for the result of that conference was the laying aside of all ceremonies, and the preaching of the plain Gospel. Let the reader reflect on the light burdens that were laid on the Gentiles. The injunction might properly be styled a command to obey the golden rule. The Gentiles were not to be burdened with Jewish ceremonies or ordinances; but in this age, if a man will not submit to the creeds and ceremonies of particular churches, he will not be acknowledged or allowed to be a Christian, though he has been one from his youth.

These dissensions are working immense mischief at present. Various Christian churches do but little else than attack and defend creeds and ceremonies, and the minister's capacity is reckoned accordingly; and so blinded have they become in this degraded warfare that they are unable to see that truth suffers, and may be lost sight of in the contest.

The Christian world have also the same superstitious veneration for their ceremonies that the Pagan idolater has for his idols: they were practised by their fathers, and are considered holy. Both Christian and Pagan idolaters are alike intolerant and even cruel; they condemn all to hell that will not worship as themselves. They cannot be taught that religion is truth, and is sanctioned by reason. How greatly will they be astonished in the resurrection when they find that God judges according to truth, justice, and reason, instead of their creeds and ceremonies! When men call warfare Christianity, then it is in danger of repudiation by the intelligent world. The very fact that this warfare exists proves the fallacy of creeds, ceremonies, &c., because they are of men, are imperfect, and subject to reprehension. God's gospel and religion is perfect, reasonable, just, and holy; and the veriest scoundrel, hypocrite, or murderer, will confess it to be so. The force of the golden rule is acknowledged by all, however vile or degraded. Confront the heathen, or savage, or idolater, with it, and he will acknowledge its binding efficacy, and apologise for its non-performance. The man that denies this rule is degraded below the brutes of earth, and is to be spurned as a thief, robber and murderer. None, however, deny its binding force; even the worst of criminals confess it, and, to excuse its requirements, all transgressors interpose the plea of necessity, or uncontrollable circumstances, for a justification of their conduct.

Here we might digress for a moment and take a glance at this excuse. This plea exists but in a very limited sense. It cannot excuse aggressive wrong, war and strife; it cannot relieve from the performance of charity. It has no force to cover the sin of pride, folly, vanity, extortion, and oppression, and these are the cases in which it is most commonly interposed. Unless we examine ourselves closely and scrutinize our conduct carefully, we are certain to be misled by this plea. It is not of heaven, but of earth, and is sensual and devilish, and without doubt more souls will be disgraced and condemned by it in eternity than by any other, save one.

The oppression of the poor and weak will, without controversy, cause more damnation in eternity than all other sins combined; this arises from an imperfect development or total absence of charity. A person may have love in some degree for the poor and weak, yet this love is not of that fervid description sufficient to counteract selfishness or the devil. From want of proper exercise love becomes faint, and the possessor then begins his oppressions of the weak and poor; covetousness seizes the place that love should occupy, and

the individual commences exacting usury and
practising extortion on that neighbor whom
he should love as himself. These acts of usury, extortion, &c., are prolific of misery, suffering, and often, remotely, of murder. They are,
as it were, missiles hurled against society.
The strong, the independent, and the preacher
stand aside and the missiles pass, and, what
is the more lamentable, the weak and helpless
become the victims: so the infant, the sick,
and helpless old age, are the chief sufferers!
The minister observes these evil practices, but
he does not consider that he is particularly
called upon to preach right and justice, but
rather to defend creeds and ceremonies. Besides, he probably knows that he has not
taught his church that such were wrong, and
that if he should trace up these malpractices
he might find that they originated in his own
flock. The same may be only too truthfully
observed of other wrongs. It is deplorable
and shameful that mankind derive but little
of their knowledge of wright and wrong, and
of love and mercy, from the preachers.

Necessity is a plea claimed alike by Christians, moralists, tyrants, robbers, and murderers. It is often interposed when there is not the least foundation for its existence. Man is too often the parent of his own necessities; his necessities are begotten by a disregard of the golden rule, and cannot justify any tortious act, nor excuse him in the performance of duty. We are not to trust this plea only when we are not at fault and when circumstances are beyond our control. It cannot be doubted that the employment of force, and even war and bloodshed, is at times justifiable under this plea; but it must be of a defensive nature, and not aggressive for the purpose of robbery and plunder, either of property or natural rights. Most of the strife and wars of mankind are prompted by a spirit of vanity and robbery. Yet, gild this chief of all villanies—aggressive war, rapine and murder—with the appellation of patriotism; beat a drum and throw a flag to the breeze, and how many Christians and professors of religion are ready to enlist for the carnage! They do not even halt to reflect on the justice of their acts, or the enormity of the deeds they are about to perpetrate. They are to be cloaked with patriotism. No difference if it is oppression, robbery, and murder—no difference if the people you assail merely claim the rights you claim and enjoy—this specious plea of patriotism is to justify you. Away with such teachings! away with such religion! for they are of the devil. What must be the degradation and shame of those men and rulers who foment strife and bloodshed among mankind—who kill, rob and plunder other nations through a spirit of vanity! Their reward can scarcely excel that of hyenas or brutes. These brutes are often cited by the christian world as exemplary and great—great because their deeds are damnable, and the injuries they have inflicted on the earth irreparable. Whence comes this false philosophy? why this false teaching? why these damnable wrongs? Simply because mankind and the ministry are teaching idle creeds and puerile ceremonies instead of the eternal truths of God. So that their dogmas are confessed and their shibboleths uttered, and so the subject exhibits a sanctimonious exterior and refrains from dancing and other amusements, the spiritual guides would send him to heaven, and bespeak for him its highest seats of glory and honor, though he was stained with extortion, oppression of the poor, and even robbery and murder. If this be religion, then religion is in vain, and of earth. Not so though, reader. We are to be judged and rewarded according to our works, and our works are the evidences of our religion. Religion is not a gift, but a duty we all owe to God, and is of life-time duration; and this duty we must perform, or suffer degradation and shame in eternity.

These ceremonies, creeds and traditions of men were severely condemned by Christ. He accused the priests and elders of imposing burdens on the people that they themselves would not touch or move with one of their fingers—of casting the moat out of their neighbor's eye while a beam was in their own—of straining at a gnat and swallowing a camel—

of making long prayers for a pretence, while they devoured widows' houses—of climbing into the sheepfold or entering heaven by ways other than the door, or obedience to the golden rule. And he reproved the Jews for divers other practices of like nature. Some say he was vindictive in his abuse. This we cannot admit. The evil of the Jewish teachings and ceremonies was great; they had misled men from the true Gospel, as now; and hence his denunciation was only adequate to the evil. The Jews were then, as the religious world is now, much wedded to creeds and ceremonies; they were neglecting the weighty matters of the law to perform these; their ceremonies were handed down, as now, from their ancestors, and were then, as now, venerated. When Christ attacked them, they considered that not only their judgment was attacked, but that he had assailed their honor, their sincerity, their religion, and their God, when in truth he had assailed naught but their follies and false teachings. He did not endeavor to condemn but to enlighten their understanding.

They considered it differently ; therefore they accused him of madness, blasphemy, and sedition, and unjustly crucified him, though he was found not guilty at least twice, if not oftener. But the Jews could not bear to have their rites and doctrines questioned, so they crucified him. Let me here again assert that his crucifixion, death, and resurrection, are no part of his religion ; but the same consists in his example and teachings, and is truth, and existed from eternity. Hence, those that obey his teachings, or the golden rule, will be saved though they never heard of Christ. He taught no sectarian religion. The belief in him is a belief of truth, and the performance of it.

I cannot dismiss this subject without a word of apology for the plain manner and candor in which I have treated it. I would not by any means have the reader believe that I am a contemner of churches, church worship, or the ministry. There is no man that more heartily approves of churches, church worship, and the ministry, than myself. While I have pointed out some errors, they are mere ciphers compared to the usefulness and benefits which they are conferring on mankind. I do not wish to be understood as questioning the sincerity of professors or teachers, and wish them abundant success. The minister is too often poorly provided for, especially if he teaches plain truths and condemns error. If the reader is a member of the church, let him remain there. Religion is perfect, but church government is not, nor need the reader expect to find perfection in any church; consequently, if he can truthfully comply with the requirements of his church, let him do so. It is the duty of all to support the church, whether members or not. Without churches and the ministry mankind would soon relapse into barbarism, and society plunge into anarchy, strife and bloodshed.

I wish further to observe that no creed, confession, or ceremony, is of any damaging nature to any individual whatever unless it is false, and false in such a manner as to cause harm to others, or evil in its nature, or causes error and wilful error by misguiding others. Many ceremonies are of the most innocent nature; others are of a wicked and superstitious nature, such as throwing infants under Juggernaut cars or "holy" vehicles, or throwing them into rivers, as a sacrifice to imaginary gods; burying women alive on the death of their husbands, and such like deeds. These should teach us to be on our guard in comply ing with superstitious ceremonies.

The whole carnal nature of man is corrupt and vicious, and is also in a state of antagonism to the principles of truth and righteousness. His carnal nature is at war with his divine nature. The first is the representative of earth and sin, while the latter is the representative of heaven and righteousness. His carnal nature is selfishness, while his divine nature is truth, justice to all, love, mercy, and holiness. The flesh prompts to evil deeds, while the spirit forbids. Shame and degradation in eternity certainly await all who disobey the teachings of the spirit and yield to carnality. This carnality, or self-worship and vanity, is so rife in the world that it must be controlled by temporal laws of society, and punished with corporeal punishment, otherwise man's existence on earth would be quite limited. This carnality is Satan unloosed, and the natural state of all the flesh of earth is war and strife, and peace the exception. Man has instituted social government in order to alleviate the sufferings ensuing from this strife and war, but has never been able to eradicate the evil. This war and strife is one of the evils of earth from which there is no escape. In vain have communities and nationalities formed compacts for peace, protection, and social security. Sin and the changes of earth sweep them away, and robbery, carnage and devastation follow. While men and nations fancy themselves in peace and security, they are probably on the threshhold of strife and death. Satan is raging and seeking whom he may devour. He exists in all flesh, rational and irrational, and is the fomenter of all strife and every evil work. A man may be ever so good and just, and ever so much inclined to peace, yet he has no assurance that his neighbor is so. Hence there arises distrust, because we

know there is an evil spirit in the world. If
this evil spirit is properly restrained by temporal laws, it begets confidence in society.
The terror of temporal punishment increases
security; but the moment this terror is relaxed, society is plunged into strife, anarchy, and
war. If we are in a country where no such
compact exists, then we can only rely on our
strength for protection. Hence, if two broth-
ers should meet in such a country and did not
recognize each other, they would naturally be
disposed to avoid a close meeting. This is
not as it should be, but proves that there is
an extraordinary vile principle in man — this
principle is self and vanity. This same principle causes brutes to fight when coming in
contact, just as it often causes men and nations. Vanity, though so often excused, is one
of the most vile and degrading passions of
earth; it is the parent of relentlessness and
revenge, and creates more wrong, misery and
suffering on earth than any other principle. It
likewise begets numerous follies and artificial
wants. In truth, mankind labor more to aug-

ment the follies of vanity than to satisfy their
natural wants.

The strife that pervades earth and the nature of man also exists in his own system or
frame. He is suspended in convulsions, in the
form of breathing, between heaven and earth
and between life and death. These convulsive
breathings are a contest between life and death.
His system cannot be understood by physicians or philosophers. Why, this convulsive
breathing, this breath of animal life, is a mys.
tery as profound as godliness itself! Why life
exists, no man can elucidate other than by
ascribing it to the direct agency of God. The
Spirit of God exists in us, giving us life, and
the moment it is withdrawn the mortal is a
wreck of ruin. This spirit of man is restless,
impatient. and full of anxious hope. It is conscious that it does not, only transiently, belong to earth. It feels as a bird entrapped,
and that it is condemned to a prison in its
fleshly tabernacle. But rend the tabernacle or
prison with violence, or wreck it with disease
and misery so as to admit its escape, and it

quits its earthly tenement and wings its flight
with the speed of thought to the God who gave
it. Here we have the resurrection of the man,
the triumph of truth, and the degradation of
the flesh. The flesh, after the spirit has taken
its everlasting leave, is then seen in its true
light, a mass of ruin and corruption. All that
was good has returned to God, there to receive
the bliss of heaven according to its works.
This was the true man; that which remains is
corruption. Hence we find some secluded spot
and commit the remains to the tomb, because
it is not our friend who has departed, but only
his infirmities. As solemn as this separation
of soul and body may be to us, it is only the
new birth of the soul in the eternal heavens,
and the putting off corruption for incorruption, of mortality for immortality; and that
man or woman who entertains the belief that
this change may be for the worse, even though
its subject be notoriously criminal, has not
sufficient faith and trust in God, whose power
is infinite and His mercy all-abounding. And
though our rewards will, and should be, pro-

portioned to our works, heaven is so pure and sublime that the least and most degraded there will excel the greatest and most exemplary of earth; at least, Christ conveys the idea; and it is so reasonable from what we do see and know, that none should dare dispute it.

CHAPTER V.
THE RESURRECTION.

REMARKS—NOT SPECIAL BUT GENERAL—EFFECTED BY NATURAL LAWS—COMBINED POWERS OF HEAVEN AND EARTH EFFECT IT—EVIDENCES OF IT—CERTAINTY OF IT—TRANSMIGRATION OF SOULS ON EARTH DENIED—EXAMPLES—VEGETATION—ANIMAL LIFE CONSCIOUSNESS—DREAMING—INNATE KNOWLEDGE OF IT—ABUNDANT LIFE OF EARTH—ABUNDANT LIFE OF HEAVEN—THE JUDGMENT—THE REWARDS—THE GOOD—THE EVIL—GOD'S BENEVOLENCE—HIS MERCY—HIS PROVISION FOR ALL.

In the last chapter we viewed the situation of man on earth, his existence, his religion, and his death and burial; we will now examine a few among the many evidences of his resurrection.

We will at the outset proceed as if we had

no Bible or revelation, and see how far nature
proves it. St. Paul says in 1st chapter of Romans, "For the invisible things of Him from
the creation of the world are clearly seen, being understood by the things that are made,
even His eternal power and Godhead; so that
they are without excuse." The heavens declare the existence of a supreme and infinite
God; they also prove that they were not made
for a vain or capricious purpose, but for the
enjoyment of beings far superior to any on
earth. The God who created them has limitless power; He gives life and existence to the
creatures of earth and to those of heaven. The
destiny of both heaven and earth is controlled
by His will, which is exerted in accordance
with laws at once perfect, just, uniform, impartial, and eternally unchanging. The motions of the heavenly bodies prove this. We
see that God has provided room for all, for
heaven is an endless infinity of planets, suns,
and emerald-like spheres, free from toil, desire, pain, misery, sorrow, tears, and death.
We know that He has power to resurrect us

all, and the only question that remains to be examined is whether He has made provision for our resurrection and enjoyment in heaven.

There are persons who believe in the transmigration of souls from one body to another here on earth. Man, it is said, has imagined that he recognized a departed relative or friend in a cat, dog, or horse. This is folly and superstition. No such thing could take place. We have instances of insects undergoing great changes in form, color, and external appearance; but life was the same in each. Changes occur also in the life of men and animals, as from infancy to manhood, and from manhood to old age and death; but the spirit is the same, and the same animating cause.

Death effects a change that is permanent and involuntary. It entirely overpowers the flesh and leaves it a mass of ruin; and when the spirit of life has once fled from the carnal body, it is free from the pains and degradation of earth, never more to return. There is an innate sense that teaches us that there is a heaven and a God, and a race of beings and an enjoyment greatly superior to earth. This sense is divine, and is the parent of fortitude and hope. It is the same that sustains and enlivens us when approaching death's door, either by disease or old age. Even when in the throes of death, it teaches that the change is not for the worse; that, though the earthly body dies, the immortal soul of man makes an eternal gain. This sense makes the old man of fourscore years as lively and hopeful, and even more cheerful, than the youth of eighteen or twenty years. In robust health, we have a great horror of death; but when reduced to a dying state, this sense of a better world and a reunion with our departed friends in heaven banishes this dread. The immortal soul begins to assert its dominion over the carnal body, for its deliverance and new birth is at hand. The great truth that death is its eternal gain, is now becoming visible. This innate sense teaches the resurrection of the dead, and is true and divine in its nature.

There is a principle in man which he derives from heaven that prompts him to believe that he and his departed friends and relatives must again meet. Hence he is on the look-out for his departed friends and relatives. He watches and searches the graveyard, the lonely places of earth, and the secret chambers, intuitively, as if but to catch a glimpse of them. He is conscious that they exist somewhere, and that their existence is of a powerful nature; hence his anxiety and search. But all his searches on earth have proved and will prove in vain, because earth is not suited to their abode; and if we get any glance of them, we must cast our eyes heavenward. There we behold a place that is not only suited, but has abundant room for our departed friends and relatives, and also for all the creatures of earth that have existed or will exist.

The reader must bear in mind that heaven embraces the whole infinity of creation, universal space, and mechanism, as exhibited in the starry firmament. Only a part, and a very small part, of heaven is thus exhibited to our eyesight. Now, the earth is one of the stars and a part of heaven, and is as a mere bubble on the ocean compared to the remainder. Many of the fixed stars, and even secondary ones, are many times larger than this earth. These planets, stars, and suns, exist through all space. Their number and boundaries and extent paralyze speech, and reduce the imagination to beggary. No human mind can conceive the limits, extent or duration of eternity and space. Thought can rapidly overcome space and count myriads of years, but the depths of eternity are beyond its powers. Now, if this architecture of God exists above, below, and all around us, as it certainly does, what is the relation of the other heavenly bodies to earth, or earth to them? Is there no communion between them? If so, it behooves us to study and ascertain this communion.

We find that there are certain elements on earth, as fire, air, earth, and water; and we further find that animal and vegetable life are approximately produced by them; that heat and cold, as they exist on earth, have apparently life-giving and life-destroying properties, which are exerted through the action of the air and the properties of earth. But the question presents itself here, can these properties of earth give or sustain life of themselves? The answer is emphatically that they cannot. They must have the assistance of the light of heaven, and also the Spirit of God. Exclude the light of heaven, and you extinguish life; withdraw the Spirit of God from the things of earth, and they are dead. So we find that there is a direct communion between this earth and heaven, and that by two of the most powerful elements known to creation— the spirit of life, and the light of heaven.

Light is a powerful element, and capable of supporting and driving the vast architecture of heaven, including this "cumbrous earth." It has properties just as air, earth, and water, only on a scale as far superior to earth as heaven is to earth. The earth is the habitation of the creatures of the air, while heaven is the habitation of the creatures of the light. Light is pure, equable, and serene; while the air is impure, boisterous, and turbulent, and unfit for the abode of angels.

But in what manner do the creatures of earth pass from earth to heaven? It is by certain organized and unerring laws of nature, and not by any partial act or providence of God. As nature and the Spirit of God placed man on earth, so will the same nature and Spirit resurrect him to eternal life. If earth can give carnal life, why not heaven give spiritual life? Heaven has multiplied more powers than earth.

Mankind are skeptical because they cannot spiritually see and discern for themselves; but man is a transgressor and a degraded being, and is not in his proper condition. If he was free from condemnation and in his true estate, there would be no necessity for the change. His condemnation is deprivation of many of his spiritual powers, such as spiritual sight and the power of locomotion or change of place at will, as we may very justly infer, and the substitution of earthly powers, such as appetite, fatigue, sense of cold, &c. Many of our powers are shorn from us, and will never be restored on this earth. Another of these powers is the divining of men's thoughts. This we have not, and are therefore the subjects of frequent impositions or cheats. There are without doubt divers others, which, if we had them, would make us equal to the angels of heaven. Because man has not the perceptive faculty to see God and the angels of heaven, nor wisdom to understand their nature, it does not prove that they do not exist. We know they do exist because their works are visible. It only proves that their existence is of a nature far more excellent and exalted than ours.

God has exhibited to us His eternal heaven, and has taught us by nature that our resurrection may be implicitly relied upon. For illustration: Plant an acorn in the soil; presently the seasons force it to swell, then burst and shoot out into the open air, and then grow and branch out to be a mighty tree, waving its branches in the air, which is an element quite different from the soil from which it sprang. It springs from the soil to the atmosphere, and is nurtured by the seasons till it becomes a mighty tree. Now, why did it vegetate, grow,

and become a tree? The reason is not known
to man, but is to be attributed to the power of
God, who gave life to the acorn. This life was
manifested by certain unerring laws. Why
will not a marble grow and become a tree?
Because it is not possessed of life, and God's
laws have no vivifying effect upon it. The
acorn grew and became a tree because it had
life in it, because it was in elements adapted
to its growth, and was nurtured properly by
seasons of moisture, rain, and heat. Man and
the creatures of earth are possessed of like life,
but on a more excellent and exalted scale, and
are surrounded with all the elements and powers necessary to their certain and speedy resurrection. I say speedy, for we are implanted
just as the acorn was, and our death or bursting forth into a new and excellent element
is at hand. The air that we breathe is the
element (not the grave, as some persist) in
which we are implanted for regeneration by
Almighty God and His angels; and this atmosphere, in which we are all embedded, combined with the germ of life within us and the

16

light and spirit of heaven above, will as certainly resurrect us and bring us into angelic life as the soil, &c., vegetated the acorn and brought the oak into the air and light of earth.

Man has life more visible than the acorn, and the amosphere has properties equal to the soil, and heaven's powers are far superior to those of earth. The acorn, after a time imbedded in the soil, swells, then bursts and decays. So with man's existence in this atmosphere: he is first an infant, then a man, and is finally bursted by death, and then springs into the angelic life of heaven. Our bodies rot and decay just as the acorn or other substances or seeds planted in the earth, because of no further use to the soul in heaven than the acorn is to the tree. Heaven will furnish us bodies, compared to which these we now enjoy are as corruption, filth, weakness, and poverty; and our works here on earth are just the same to our future welfare as the roots and good soil are to the oak—let them be good and thrifty, or weak and poor. The soil in which the acorn is implanted is shallow and easily affected by

the seasons of earth ; so is also the atmosphere
in which we are implanted likewise shallow,
comparatively speaking. The seasons of earth
bring forth the acorn to a newness of life ; so
the powers of heaven, such as light, the Spirit
of God, and vivifying properties of heaven, being in immediate contact with our bodies and
immortal souls, will as certainly resurrect us
into the newness of angelic life. We see and
know that we are in contact with these powers
of heaven and that we have our life from them,
for no power on earth can for a moment give
or sustain life ; yet because our mortal frames
die and rot as the acorn, we seem to doubt.
Did not the offspring of the acorn, the mighty
oak, quit the soil in which it was imbedded,
and that caused it to sprout, and then wave its
towering branches in a purer element? So
also will man's new birth be a resurrection in
an element as far excelling the atmosphere of
earth as the atmosphere excels the filthy soil
of earth. Man is far superior to the acorn or
vegetable life ; and because he branches forth
to a purer and more noble and exalted exist-

ence than is found in the strife and turmoil of earth, and becomes to us invisible, is not by any means a proof that he is spiritually dead.

The worms of the dirt change their forms and places of existence. It would seem quite impossible, if we did not know the fact from observation, that they should quit the slime of the soil and come out and enjoy the atmosphere as winged insects, flying from object to object. Now, if God is so merciful and condescending as to notice and provide for the enjoyment of these creatures of the slime and dirt, why should mankind despair or doubt? These creatures of the slime can neither praise nor worship Him, yet He cares enough for them to give them a higher existence, and thus at the same time teach man that His providence and benevolence extend not only to him, but to all the creatures of the earth, however insignificant. God does not govern the world through caprice, but by uniform and impartial laws; hence every creature possessing His spirit of life must be resurrected to the enjoyment of heaven. Heaven has room and appropriate enjoyments for all that ever was, is, or shall be; so all must prepare, both small and great, for the resurrection and newness of life. This earth is but the temporary abode of man and other living creatures, made or adopted on design for two purposes: first, for instruction and repentance to God; and secondly, for regeneration into heaven. It has the necessary commotions, changes and strife to effect both, and death and the resurrection are laws of nature and must transpire: the one is just as certain as the other—one results from the other.

It seems, however, with some skeptics an impossibility for man to enjoy life only in one element—that is, the air—or in any body except a corporeal one; but if we will examine the nature of life, we find by our own senses that it exists in different elements. Here on the surface of the earth is man, the animals, and winged tribes, enjoying life in the air. In the water of the seas and rivers we find whales, fishes, lobsters, and even the little corals, enjoying life. The life they enjoy is in a differ-

ent element, and is to us a mystery. In the
dirt and slime of earth we find the worms and
insects enjoying life; and to add still further
evidence, when the earth is penetrated we find
occasionally frogs (live frogs) imbedded in
solid rock far beneath the surface of the earth,
and in positions where they must have remained for centuries. These frogs are not
dead, but have been secluded from the strife
of earth and the regenerating properties of
heaven; for when brought in contact with
these they assume or exhibit visible life. Neither death nor the resurrection would have
any effect on these entombed frogs; but God,
in due time, by the vicissitudes of earth, will
finally disinter and resurrect them. These
facts prove beyond a doubt that life does exist, and can exist, in any element of earth, and
that it does and can exist in heaven. There
are angels or children of light, as well as men
and animals of the air, fishes and corals of the
sea and water, and worms and insects of the
dust and soil. One life is just as possible with
God as another, and reason forbids that we

should assume that God made the starry heavens and firmament, and all the host of them, for no purpose except for the poor mortals of earth to look and wonder at.

But says one, why do we not see God and His angels? The answer is, we are not yet the children of light. We are of earth, and our carnal nature is earthly, and we are spiritually blind. We know that like begets like, and that everything yields and brings forth after its kind. Hence the inhabitants and things of earth have those properties and character engrafted on them; they have a corporeal nature, as air, water, soil, flesh, trees, grass, &c. But the light of heaven is of quite a different nature from that of earth. It is seen, but is seen mysteriously. We might say or conclude that, because we cannot comprehend its nature, it cannot be seen. We know it exists because we do see it. Now the products of light are of the same purity and nature as light itself, just as the products of earth partake of its nature. Hence, as we do not understand the nature of light, we cannot see or comprehend the nature of angelic life. It is spiritual and substantial, and far more potent and glorious than any of earth; and the mechanism of the starry heavens is the abode of God and His angels of light.

Carnal life is weak and fleeting, spiritual life is powerful and eternal. We behold the heavens with our natural eyes, and see a wonderful and sublime creation far superior to earth or anything conceivable by man. It is alone conclusive proof that there is a high state of existence beyond earth and the grave. The vast architecture of heaven is not a myth or delusion placed before our eyes, but a certain reality, and is truth.

Our learned men have demonstrated to a certainty that many of the stars and planets of heaven are many times larger than our earth; that the sun which gives us light is several hundred thousand times larger than our globe; that some of the fixed stars are many trillions of miles from us. The planetary systems of heaven are perfect, and are working in the most admirable harmony; they are governed by laws that know no change. Owing to the great distance these heavenly bodies are placed from us, we could not see the workings and existence of their inhabitants even if they were corporeal as we. This great distance is seemingly an obstacle not easily overcome; but spiritual beings can conquer distance as fast as the human mind can conceive, and as quick as thought can penetrate. If, while in our degraded or infantile state, we could see these beings, we could not comprehend their nature. No reasonable mind can doubt the existence of God and the celestial spheres which God called "heaven," nor can we doubt the existence of angels. The spiritual body is quite different to this mortal one, though in form and shape like it. It is not a phantom or myth, but a sublime and powerful existence, of the true nature of which we are still ignorant, and must exercise patience till all future things are unvailed and the mysteries of heaven revealed in the resurrection. Time and the resurrection will certainly develop in us a glorious and powerful existence as our works deserve. St. John in Revelations represents four angels standing on the four corners of the earth, and holding the four winds; another as having the seal of the living God; that he saw "a mighty angel come down from heaven, clothed with a cloud; and a rainbow was upon his head, and his face was as it were the sun, and his feets as pillars of fire: and he had in his hand a little book open: and he set his right foot upon the sea, and his left foot on the earth, and cried with a loud voice, as when a lion roareth," &c. Again he represents angels as pouring vials of wrath upon the earth and sun; another as illuminating the earth with his glory. He represents another as coming down from heaven with the key of the bottomless pit, and having power to lay hold of the dragon, &c. From these we are to infer that angelic life will not be deficient in glory and power. Reason teaches, aside from revelation, that it will be glorious and powerful. From the foregoing scriptural quotations we are forced to admit that there are different grades of existence and power in heaven, for St. John speaks of "angels," and also of "powerful angels." These differences are taught in the Scriptures, and are sanctioned by reason and justice, and may therefore be considered as truths.

Man's spiritual life now existing in him is immortal, and the direct gift of heaven, and cannot die. It will leave this terrestrial body, and should do so, because the earth and the creatures thereof are corrupt, and is not the eternal home of any. Death, though regarded as a terror and disaster, and dreaded as such, is an everlasting triumph of the soul. Truth, by it, prevails over error, good over evil, and the spirit over the flesh. By this triumph error is subdued, so also is desire, pain, sickness, hunger, thirst, fatigue, sorrow, tears, and death, all done away and banished forever; while love, joy, peace, good-will, and the glory of heaven, abound in their stead. "Death," says St. Paul, "will be swallowed up in victory."

The fact that man possesses an innate knowledge of again meeting his friends and relatives beyond the grave is proof of the resurrection. Man has an anxiety to meet them again, and is constantly on the alert for a sight of them. This feeling and consciousness is not of earth, but is the gift of heaven, and a warning to the soul within to prepare for our departure. It is from heaven, and this consciousness and warning is truth. Error is of earth, and prompts men to think otherwise; but God has not only set the truth before our eyes, but He has implanted it in our souls. So when we discover the truth that heaven exists, and also feel the truth that we must depart from earth and meet our God and redeemed friends, we should act accordingly.

The birds of the air seem desirous of instructing man that there is a higher enjoyment above. They sail through the air with great rapidity and ease, as if to show man that he was not in his true home, as if heaven was above and at his command. Man sees that they can fly through the air, and finds also that they are adapted so as to be able to do so, and there contents himself to stop. But go a little farther, if you please. Who so made them? who enabled them to accomplish such feats? Of course, the power that can call into being all the visible works of the created heavens and earth is omnipotent, and can and will resurrect and give life in heaven.

God teaches life and the resurrection in various ways. The indestructibility of the soul is also proved by dreaming. In a state of sleep the powers of animal life are in some measure suspended; they become overpowered by fatigue and exertion, and seek repose, and the animal powers become more or less unconscious. During this repose the soul or spirit of the sleeper is not so wearied and fatigued, not being subject to such infirmities, but steals off from the body, as it were, and often traverses and roams through an immense amount of time and space. It probably will, if not annoyed by the suffering of the flesh or sleeping body, visit scenes and countries thousands of miles away, and even cross oceans. Some of these dreams are of a pleasant nature, depending on the comfort of the body and health of the sleeper. When the body is free from pain, suffering, and want, our dreams are of the most pleasing description; if the body is in pain, surfeit, want, &c., our dreams are unpleasant and often frightful, so close are the mind and body interwoven with each other. The soul and body being thus closely blended, the tortures of the body trouble and vex the soul, and it is never entirely freed from these until death relieves it. When the body is entirely free from pain, want, and suffering, and subjected to quiet sleep, then our dreams become highly pleasant; our spirits will often recur to scenes of childhood, and visit mountain tops and view the most beautiful and sublime scenery: this scenery sometimes becomes holy and enchanting, and this when the mind is not yet free, but subject to the ills of the flesh. Now, if the soul is once freed from this evil, suffering body, and endowed with one that is not subject to the infirmities of the flesh, what must be the enjoyment of that soul! It certainly would surpass any of this earth, and would convey an approximate idea of the beatific enjoyment and happiness of heaven.

Our bodies, as all know, are mortal and subject to death; they are not of a heavenly nature, and die because offensive to heaven and unpleasing in the sight of God and His angels. The spirit is of God, and must return. God in His mercy and wisdom has provided for a return to Him of all the inhabitants of this earth, both rational and irrational, that possess His Spirit, whether they be creatures of the air, water, or soil. Some small creatures are, no doubt, first enlarged into a higher existence on earth, imperceptibly to man. It is absurd and selfish in man to deny the resurrection of the smaller and irrational beings of earth. They are existing by God's help and Spirit, and are subject to want. pain, hunger, and death, just as man; and the same omnipotent and benevolent God that created them will as certainly resurrect them also to a higher existence. Heaven is not a limited space for the sanctimonious few, but embraces God's creation, and has ample room and appropriate enjoyments for all, however debased or insignificant, or however excellent and exalted. Then, why deny the resurrection and resplendent glory of heaven to any, whether rational as man, or irrational as the beasts, birds, fishes, &c.? They are all the creatures of God, and exist by His will, and are subject to the same laws that must resurrect all. Time and the force of these laws will soon waft the whole into the bliss of eternity. God has taught us by nature that He can give life in the air, life in the water, and life in the dust of earth. He has taught us that this life can spring from one element to another. He exhibits to us the mechanism and sublimity of heaven in an element the most pure, serene, and powerful of all—the light of heaven. He has taught us the immediate connection existing between heaven and earth by means of this light and the spirit which He has given us. He has shown us that He has provided for all both in earth and heaven, and why doubt our redemption and resurrection? It is but to doubt our own senses. Why do we hope for that which we see? Heaven and eternal life is in sight, and our redemption and resurrection at hand. St. James tells us that "the Judge standeth before the door." St. John tells us that "His reward is with Him, to give to every man according as his works shall be." He says further, "And I heard a voice from heaven saying unto me, Write, Blessed *are* the dead which die in the Lord from henceforth: yea, saith the Spirit, that they may rest from their labors; and their works do follow them." From these Scriptures, and the philosophy already advanced, there is to be no slumbering in the grave, as many suppose. The spirit of man never enters that dismal abode, but when it passes the door of death it instantly wings its eternal flight to God. As the things of earth disappear and fade away in the hour of death, so the sublimity and glory of heaven come in view. As we take leave of our friends on earth we must be ready to salute our redeemed friends and the angels in heaven. Death but calls us from one to the other: it is the summons to change positions and friends. While

17

we leave a few friends to mourn our loss on earth, how innumerably more stand ready to rejoice because of our redemption in heaven! Those behind must follow, and thus the entire heavens be enlivened with the whole of God's creatures.

As to the nature of heaven, we have some light both by observation and by revelation; and, in this instance, observation and reason are quite consonant with the teachings of the Bible. The Bible teaches that there is a difference in the future existence and enjoyment of man; reason and justice teach that there should be. The heavenly bodies show that they are of different grades or sizes, and are differently illuminated, and in all probability adapted to the comfort and enjoyment of all classes, persuasions, and conditions of life, as their merits deserve. St. Paul, in 1 Cor. xv., gives a true picture of the resurrection and its nature; he says, "There are also celestial bodies, and bodies terrestrial: but the glory of the celestial is one, and the glory of the terrestrial is another. There is one glory of the sun and another glory of the moon, and another glory of the stars: for one star differeth from another star in glory. So also is the resurrection of the dead. It is sown in corruption; it is raised in incorruption. It is sown in dishonor; it is raised in glory. It is sown in weakness; it is raised in power. It is sown a natural body; it is raised a spiritual body. * * * Now this I say, brethren, that flesh and blood cannot inherit the kingdom of God." So says St. Paul, and his statements are to be implicitly relied on, for he has reason and truth on his side. Besides, he gives us to understand that he was caught up into the third heaven, and saw things not lawful for a man to utter. (See 2 Cor. xii.) Without doubt, St. Paul's spiritual sight was opened when he was so miraculously converted; as also other of the apostles: and when they testified of these facts, and yielded up their lives as martyrs to the truth of their assertions, mankind should not be skeptical, more especially when corroborated by reason and observation.

It seems from this that heaven is classed

into three different grades at least; and how many different enjoyments may be assigned to each is to us not now important, as we may confidently rely that the most impartial justice will be done us, and each rewarded, and amply rewarded, according as his work shall be. We see for ourselves, however, that a difference exists in the sidereal heavens, and St. Paul informs us that this difference will exist in the resurrection. Without the least doubt heaven has many grades, varieties, and differences, as earth itself, with the exception of sin, evil, death, &c. We may also conclude that it has select portions, where Christ and his angels will enjoy themselves. This portion is attained only by the straight and narrow way, the "golden rule," and the great bulk of mankind will be excluded from its enjoyment because they have fallen short of its requirements, and from the highest grade enjoyed by the elect. We shall probably find that the grades recede from one to another in such order as to reward each and every one as their works deserve; but, as heaven is pure and good and free from death, all will be benefited by the change, though they suffer what the Bible terms "damnation," "damnation the greater," "hell," "hell-fire," "fiery furnace," and "the lake that burneth with fire and brimstone." These are mere figures of speech, and were simply intended to convey the idea that man must be rewarded according to his works. "Damnation" only represents the falling short of the glory of God. "Hell," "hell-fire," &c., represent the loss of the better estates and ranks which in God's providence were designed for the subject. St. John was a preacher of this doctrine, probably more so than any other biblical writer, and, before he dismisses this subject of punishment, he informs us where it is to be inflicted. In Revelations, chapter 14, in speaking of those that worshipped the beast, he says, "The same shall drink of the wine of the wrath of God, which is poured out without mixture into the cup of His indignation, and he shall be tormented with fire and brimstone in the presence of the holy angels, and in the presence of the Lamb." Here we have the place before the throne of God, in the presence of the angels and the Lamb. So also with the parable of the rich man and Lazarus, taught by our Saviour. The rich man was punished in sight of heaven. The words "afar off" mean that Abraham and Lazarus had attained a rank far more excellent than his, and the "impassable gulf" signifies the impossibility of changing conditions in heaven; his "torment" was the shame and degradation to which he was justly subjected, or, in truth, to which he had subjected himself; the "smoke" represents shame, and "fire," &c., the attendant loss and degradation, which was apparent by the splendor of heaven: splendor is represented by "fire" in the Scriptures.

This is the most rational view, and is entirely consistent with the Bible All must be resurrected , and enjoy the same heaven, and receive the same rewards, according to their works. Abraham and the rich man were within conversing distance. God is no tyrant, and has not the least enmity against the world, and it is the height of absurdity to suppose

that He would subject any mortal to the men-
tal anguish and physical pain and misery of
this earth, and annihilate his body by death,
and then punish in hell-fire the only good and
righteous portion left, that is, his immortal
soul. Such is sheer folly, and is not to be believed for a moment; but such language is
and may be used to denote the loss or shame
and degradation to which the wicked subject
themselves by disobedience to God's holy law,
for it is a quite convenient way of expressing
it. The testing of works by fire, and casting
into fire, &c., is typical of subjecting the soul
to the powerful splendor of heavenly light.
This light will penetrate our very souls and
existence, and shine within them so as to dis-
close every deed and thought, whether it be
good or evil. The wicked will dread to have
their acts tested by it; hence the wailing and
gnashing of teeth, the everlasting torment, &c.,
for it would be futile to seek darkness in
heaven. I think, however, that I have satis-
factorily proved in the chapter on "Earth" (to
which the reader is referred), that fire is an

element of strife, and does not exist outside of our atmosphere, and it is improbable that such compound as the air we breathe exists anywhere else; if so, all the evils of earth exist elsewhere, which is not probable, as Moses says all was good at the bginning; and is yet so without doubt, except this earth.

In the expansive heavens there is a Paradise spoken of by our Saviour while on the cross, and it would seem to be the first place we will enter after death. Here, very likely, each one will be nurtured and schooled in the mysteries of heaven before appearing with full angelic vigor and privileges. Doubtless we may improve our spiritual knowledge and strength here in life by religious and moral culture, and, of course, our future estate and happiness depend upon it; but it is scarcely possible that mankind will enter heaven fully developed as they will be in the course of time. They may improve the state or rank to which they are admitted while on earth, but cannot so improve as to change entirely from one rank to another after the resurrection, for this would annul the judgment of God and of heaven.

Before entering heaven, man and all other beings are first deprived, by death, of all desire and power to do evil or harm. Death has slain hunger, thirst, pain, desire, misery, and death. Tears and sorrow are all wiped away, and life and happiness reign forever. We carry none of our infirmities there; only the spiritual part can be admitted. There is no guile or deceit there. "By their fruits shall ye know them." Our works follow us so completely that the least there can accurately judge us. Our acts and conduct in life are as visibly stamped on us as the founder casts his impressions on his wares; and are not only so visibly stamped, but they are stamped with the certainty that like begets like, and that everything yields or brings forth after its kind. Our thoughts are also comprehended, and no deception is there. Our works are incorporated into and form our heavenly existence. "A corrupt tree cannot bring forth good fruit." As our works are so shall our existence in heaven be, whether to our glory or shame, to our honor or dishonor.

Man's conduct on earth effectually controls the result of his judgment, and his judgment transpires on his entrance into heaven. The day of death is the day when both small and great are to be judged. Generation after generation have been judged as death called them to the bar of God, and there is no slumbering in the grave for judgment. Death is the great day mentioned in the Bible, and life is the place where we are reserved for judgment. At this bar of the living God we must all appear. Here the righteous, with their works of love, humility, self-denial, and charity—those that have endured great tribulations for truth and holiness—those that have meekly and tenderly discharged their duty to the weak and suffering poor, and those that have unostentatiously pursued the straight and narrow way of the golden rule,—will hear the welcome plaudit, " Well done, good and faithful servants," and be welcomed to the most excellent and select portion of heaven.

Then comes the moral man, who has been cautious and circumspect in his deportment while on earth, but, as he has neglected some charities and other christian duties imposed upon him by the golden rule, he is of necessity and right assigned a position and rank inferior to those who have strictly obeyed the commands; hence his rank in heaven will not be of the elect order of Christ and his angels.

Next comes the idolater with his confessions of error, which are now glaringly manifest; but as his offence is mainly attributed to ignorance and false teachings, and therefore of a pardonable nature, he is forgiven, and an estate bestowed on him far more worthy than he anticipated.

Now comes a group of virgins, arrayed for the great wedding feast: they have lamps, but only a part of them have their lamps well filled with the oil of charity; these latter have ministered to the sick and poor, fed the hungry, clothed the naked, had mercy on the orphan and poor, entertained the stranger, and therefore receive a joyful welcome, and advance to the exalted position occupied by the Redeemer and his elect angels. Not so with the other virgins who have no oil in their vessels. They had been neglectful of christian duties on earth; they had failed to entertain the stranger, visit the sick, relieve the poor, feed the hungry, or clothe the naked. While their poor neighbors were suffering for the plainest food and clothing, they were gormandizing the most sumptuous dainties, and gadding about in the most fantastical, costly and useless apparel. While the orphan and the sick required their help and attention, they were reading trashy literature and novels, and frisking about ball-rooms and flirting in wine parties. Instead of adorning true womanhood, they have disgraced it, and now appear as a group of simpletons. Heaven almost cringes, but the Judge shall condemn them for want of common sense. He, however, quickly sees the situation, and sends these foolish virgins out where they can amuse themselves in hopping and fluttering about along with the grasshoppers and June bugs.

Next comes the hypocrite, with his deception all emblazoned on him indelibly as the mark of Cain. He, no doubt, would gladly avoid the judgment-bar, but is arraigned, and must be judged. He is scarcely worth judging, but, as his shame and disgrace are so visible and contemptible, he is immediately ordered off to some remote part of the kingdom where he will not further offend the saints by his presence. This is the identical place he desired, and he takes his departure praising God for the first time for His mercy and good judgment.

Now come the false teachers : they advance with confident step and claim the inheritance of the elect. The Judge refuses to recognize them as his, and orders them to depart. Not so, however, with hem; they wish to reason the case   God must be wrong and they right. They ask, "Lord, Lord, have we not prophesied in thy name? (certainly prophesied that no one could enter the kingdom of heaven except by confessing their creeds and performing their ceremonies) and in thy name have cast out devils? (yes, cast out "poor devils" from their lands, houses, and churches, because they were unable to pay the rents or charges) and in thy name done many wonderful works?" (such, for instance, as exalting themselves in the eyes of the ignorant, attiring themselves pompously, and faring sumptuously and sometimes gluttonously, while the poor disciples and their neighbors had neither comfortable shelter, food, or raiment; and taught senseless creeds and meaningless ceremonies rather than God's Gospel of truth, love, and mercy.) Is it to be wondered that they shall fail to receive the elect's portion? So they receive the command, "Depart from me, ye that work iniquity."

Now come a multitude of all manner of sinners, consisting of liars, drunkards, usurers, extortioners, oppressors of the poor, adulterers, robbers, thieves, and murderers. They all appear before the throne, and each receives his reward as his works deserve. They are more sensible than some preachers supposed them to be; for on investigation it is found that they have compounded with each other, and so completely forgiven each other's transgressions on earth, that the Judge is disposed to be quite lenient with most of them. So he degrades none so very low, only the abominable murderers and promoters of war and strife; he marks them with the blackness of darkness, and sends them along with the ravenous beasts. The wicked are cut off in their ways, and stand here without their occupations. Money making, usury, extortion, gluttony, oppression of the poor and weak, and all other vices, find no place in heaven.

Thus all humanity must appear and receive judgment as their works shall deserve. The judgment is lenient and the rewards pleasant to each and all. No dissatisfaction will exist, and all will feel satisfied with the result; hence the heavens will echo with shouts of joy and songs of praise to Almighty God for His beneficence and mercy. There can be but little doubt that mankind and the creatures of earth will be utterly astonished at the exalted and glorious condition of heaven, and with the munificent provision a benevolent God has provided for them. But, as it is written, "Eye hath not seen, nor ear heard, neither have entered into the heart of man, the things which God hath prepared for them that love him." Here every work will meet its own reward, and every taste and condition be satisfied. Our rank and power will be apportioned to our several wants. Some will appear degraded, and this by their own conduct, not by their Creator, and others will appear exalted. To whom much was given much was required; to whom little was given little was required. The measure of each one's capacity will be full; while the capacity of some is abundant, those of others will be meagre. The places of enjoyment of all will be just such as they would naturally have chosen if left free to choose for themselves, though it may be the least desirable. Hence the universal peace, harmony and good-will of heaven; hence the love, and mercy, and happiness, of the saints in glory.

These things are not vain phantoms or idle dreams, but stern, real truths—just as certain as the light of earth proceeds from the sun, moon and stars—just as certain as the heavens exist—just as certain and sure as we live, move, and have our being on earth—just as certain will the God of the Universe, by certain unerring laws of nature, resurrect all His living creatures to a high, glorious and eternal life in heaven, where all will be rewarded as their works shall be. Revelation teaches the resurrection; nature teaches it through all of her works; man's holy spirit teaches and admonishes him of the fact, and our eyes behold our future home spread out in the heavens, and why deny our own senses? We had quite as well deny our own existence. So sure as our mortal bodies die, just so sure will our immortal souls be resurrected in heaven. They take immediate flight to heaven on the death of our carnal bodies, never to return to the strife and sin of the world.

After his friends are departed and their remains consigned to the tomb, man watches intuitively for their return, if but to catch a glimpse of the departed. He is conscious of a

18

reunion with his friends. But as time advances he sees no visible trace of his friend or relative, who may have been to him the most dear on earth. He has watched in every possible place where any trace of that friend might be found; he has visited the graveyard and the silent tomb; he has looked in the secret chambers and the lonely places of earth, but finds not the lest vestige of his departed friend. In his reflections and disappointments he too often loses hope; despair seizes his mind; his soul grows weary, and he yields to despondency and gloom, and often to lamentation and weeping. His search has been in vain because it has been amiss—he has not yet looked heavenward. Instead of searching the graveyards, tombs, secret chambers, and lonely places of earth, he should have cast his thoughts heavenward, and pursued his inquiries there. There he might have beheld the starry heavens all testifying, in a matter admitting of no guile, that God and his friends are there; they testify that He is able to save, and that there is room for all; they testify that heaven is adapted to all classes and conditions, and so pure that angels might worship in their snowy white garments through all eternity without soiling them in the least. Why not look there for our departed friends? God has power to give them life there as well as on earth. He has given life to man and animals on the land, to the fishes and corals in the sea, to the fowls of the air, to the worms and insects of the dust, to the trees of the forest and flowers of the field. He has given life in innumerable ways—earth teems with life in nearly every conceivable manner. He has given life in flesh and blood—He has given another life in vegetation—He has given another life to the corals of the sea, and another to the worms of the dust and the insects of the air; and why doubt that He will give life to His creatures in heaven, the most sublime part of His creation? The earth, air, and water, are abounding in life—life of every nature, and of every form imaginable—and why should God give life and protection to the little creatures of earth and the corals of the sea, and deny it to man, the most exalted of all His creatures of earth? The idea is absurd. With us the resurrection is a matter not remote.

Heaven also teems with angelic life. The powers of heaven are attracting and pleasingly inviting us there; the elements of earth are buffeting us, and bid us go; and time will soon waft us all into the resurrection of heaven, where all will enjoy the reward suited to their works. This change is not distant. With many of us the day is far spent, and the night cometh when no man can work. While it is yet light it behooves us all so to work that our estate in the resurrection may be ample, and our inheritance one of everlasting joy and peace.

———

CHAPTER VI.
THE MILLENNIUM.

ITS OCCURRENCE—ITS COURSE—STRIFE OF EARTH TO BE FIRST SUB-
DUED—THE WAY PREPARED BY A CELESTIAL BODY—BINDING
OF SATAN—PEACE OF EARTH—SECOND ADVENT—THE GOSPEL
TRUTH AGAIN PREACHED—PASSAGE OF THE CELESTIAL VISIT-
ANT AND DISAPPEARANCE OF CHRIST AND HIS ANGELS—SATAN
UNBOUND—THE WORLD AFTERWARDS—FORMER MILLENNIUMS
—BIBLE PROOFS—MYSTERIES OF HEAVEN REVEALED—TIME OF
IT UNKNOWN—ALL PROPHECY FALSE AS TO THE TIME.

Much has been written on this subject, and it has attracted the attention of mankind at various times. Many have been the prophecies that have proven false, and many, perhaps, will be made in the future which time will prove equally false. That there will occur a great millennial sabbath at some future period, during which Christ and his angels will visit this earth in glory and power, is plainly announced in Revelations and also positively affirmed by Christ himself. When we consider that this event may be brought about, or the way prepared, in the ordinary administration of God's immutable laws, without the intervention of any partiality or miraculous visitation of God, then we have no right to dispute the word of Christ or the teachings of Revelation.

This event will occur, not as a miracle, or by the partial favor of God, but by a fixed principle of the laws of nature, established at the creation of the heavens and earth; and it may be truthfully affirmed that millennial periods have formerly occurred, and will again and again occur, in the lengths of eternity, by the same laws of nature. How it may occur, the cause of its occurrence, and the effects produced by it, together with some remarks as to its time and duration, we will now proceed to examine.

In order to make an intelligent illustration, and view this subject rationally, we must necessarily review many of the positions heretofore assumed, without which the reader will fail to understand my views of the subject.

The first of these positions was that the whole starry firmament, as exhibited to our natural eyesight, is heaven, and was so called by God himself in the first chapter of Genesis; that this heaven is the abode of God and His angels, and embraces an eternity of time, space, and mechanism, such as stars, suns and adamantine globes, which exist indefinitely above, around, and in all directions; that these are the mansions of God and the angels, and that the earth is an integral part of this mechanism of heaven, and has its offices to perform in like manner as the others.

The second was that this earth is laboring under a curse for man's transgression, which is affirmed by the Bible, and is confirmed by observation, reason, and experience. The earth being accursed of God, its whole elements—as air, water, fire, and earth—are in a state of constant strife, war, and turmoil; and is unfit, by reason of the same, for the abode of God and His angels, or even a visit by them. This war and strife is carried into the system and nature of man, causing error, sin, misery, pain and death, and therefore rendering the earth distasteful to heavenly beings. The world and the flesh thereof are sinful and evil, and proved to be so; and therefore objectionable to pure and holy beings, who do not, and will not, visit this earth while such repulsive evils exist.

The third was that all flesh and objects of a terrestrial nature having life were the result of the changes of the elements of earth; that the flesh and animal life of men, beasts, birds, fishes, &c., result from these changes, which are all approximately caused by our atmosphere; that death also ensues from the same causes. Our carnal bodies are at enmity with God, and must die, because they are impure, unholy, and not suitable for the eternal abode of man's holy spirit. The earth also being accursed, is likewise not fit for the permanent abode of man and the creatures of earth, much less God and His angels; consequently, it is deserted by them, and has been for centuries. Hence this earth is governed by God and His angels by certain definite laws exerted from the throne of heaven, and these laws never change, but may be suspended, or seemingly suspended, by the exercise of other superior laws; all, however, work in regular and harmonious order. The workings of nature are thus diversified, and the heavens rendered interesting to the saints.

The reader must also bear in mind that I not only acknowledge a communion of spirits between heaven and earth, but have stoutly contended that we owe our very existence and life to it. That the Spirit of God dwells in us all, giving us life and reason, and to that extent we are divine ; but not so divine as Christ, for he possessed spiritual powers not enjoyed by us. We are also in direct communion with heaven by means of light, which is the most powerful element of heaven, and capable of supporting weighty and immense worlds. This light, because we cannot comprehend its powers, is not noted as an element by our philosophers, on the same principle that a fish or worm would not note our atmosphere an element because they are ignorant of most of its properties.

The strife of earth extends as far as our atmosphere, which, it will be remembered, was stated to be from thirty-nine to forty-eight miles in height from the earth's surface. This strife exists in the sea and in the bowels of the earth, causing upheavals and eruptions by the action of fire, air, water, and combustible materials. It exists in the air, causing heat, cold, rain, evaporation, perspiration, &c., which immediately cause thirst, hunger, pain, disease, decay, and death.

This strife of the earth produces changes, from which result, first, animal and vegetable life; then disease, decay, and death. This strife results from the influence of the sun and the heavenly bodies on the atmosphere of the earth. In other words, if our atmosphere had not existed and encircled the earth, there would have been no strife on earth—neither pain, misery, desire, disease, nor death. Its inhabitants would have been different and of a higher order of being. Consequently, it may be asserted that the storms and vicissitudes of our atmosphere cause all the ills and sins of earth. Where there is no strife, there is no decay, nor death; and where there is strife, there is sin, disease, decay, and death.

God forbade Adam to partake of the fruit

of the tree of the knowledge of good and evil, which is but a type of the sin and folly of earth; so He also forbade His angels to visit it. Christ visited it; but the penalty of death was attached, even to a dutiful and beloved son. Angels do not visit this earth in person or proper powers: they are not non-entities or shadows, but powerful beings, capable of producing tremendous results. Saint John speaks of "angels" and "mighty angels," and one of which he describes "chaining the dragon"; another as "standing with one foot on the land and the other on the sea"; others as "standing on the four corners of the earth, and holding the four winds." Great power is ascribed to all of them, and reason would teach that they are not phantoms, for the heavens and its powerful architecture are witnesses to the contrary. It cannot be claimed that this earth receives any of these visits, and it cannot rationally be accounted for, only by the fact that it is under the displeasure and curse of God.

Earth, as before stated, is a place fitted for

man's regeneration and atonement for offences
committed against God. Mankind's primitive
estate was heaven, which is the true Eden of the
Scripture, and for our transgressions there we
are suffering God's displeasure on earth, and
undergoing penance and regeneration. Earth
is of a two-fold nature, first teaching repentance and obedience to God, and also causing
regeneration and resurrection to life eternal in
heaven.

Sin and corruption only exist on this earth,
and result from the curse of God. The strife
results from the light of heaven making war
on the sin and corruption of earth, as truth
makes war upon error. This strife is daily,
hourly, and each moment, caused by the light
and sunbeams of heaven : they enter our atmosphere, displace its particles, cause strife
and friction, thus producing heat; and heat
and cold effect all the changes visible on earth.
Our atmosphere becomes rarefied by heat, and
when rarefied (being possessed of quite an
elastic nature) is displaced by cooler and
heavier air from its vicinity · this causes mo-

tion, called wind. When seemingly still, it absorbs perspiration from our bodies, acts on our lungs and intestines, causing thirst, pain, hunger, disease, decay, and finally death. It has by its power over the other elements of earth wrought all the changes we behold on earth. Aside from it, no filth, dirt, slime, or corruption, could have existed on the earth, but it would have been as neat and cleanly polished as a diamond, and so pure that angels might have inhabited it, and worshipped God through the eternal ages, without soiling their white garments in the least.

This strife is the approximate cause of all our ills and troubles. But why should it be so ordained that there will not even be a temporary cessation of the same, and peace reign on earth for a season? Why not suspend this strife periodically, and substitute the peace, love, and good-will of heaven, till benighted man can see the truth of heaven? The ancients profess to have witnessed these truths, and undoubtedly did, but which, of necessity, were recorded imperfectly and in figurative language.   Why should not the world, in the future, enjoy this peace, and again hear the truth of God, and see some some of the mysteries of heaven unfolded?

This strife, sin, desire, pain, and death of earth must first be banished or suspended before Christ or any of the saints of heaven visit it; and just so soon, and no sooner, may we look for the millennium, and the appearance or second advent of Christ and his angels, and their sojourn on earth will not be one moment longer than this peace reigns: they are children of peace and light, and visit no other places.   This peace and light must first come, then Christ and the redeemed of earth.   The way must be prepared for their advent on earth.

Let us suppose some mighty power should say to the elements of earth, "Peace, be still!" and that these warring elements should obey and assume a state of profound peace—what would be the results on earth?   The first and most notable effect would be the cleansing of the atmosphere; all clouds, dust, vapors, and impurities, would settle on the earth as quickly as they could fall by the force of gravitation; evaporation and absorption would cease, and thus a clear, brilliant and serene state of the atmosphere would ensue, which would become doubly resplendent by the rays of vivid light pouring down from heaven. Heat and cold would be banished or disappear, because they result from strife of the elements. Perspiration, absorption, and excretion, of the flesh and vegetation would cease; consequently, hunger, thirst, pain, desire, decay, sin, and death, would be suspended or banished, and, with them, all the evil passions known to men and beasts. There would not be the least desire for food, drink, raiment, or shelter: and no incentive to do wrong or offer violence on the part of any; hence the lion and lamb, or the hyena and little child, or the fox and the fowl, all might live and room together in the same enclosure without fear or the least apprehension of violence or danger from each other. No want would be felt of anything of earth; the animal passions and desires would

all be banished or suspended, and sin overcome; and hence Satan would be chained, as
represented in the Scriptures.

But it may be said that man and the carnality of earth would in that event cease to live,
and would sink to the earth as so many corp-
ses.   Not so, however, by any means.   Their
animal desires and powers of eating, drinking,
sleeping, and sense of cold and heat, would
only be suspended by this serene, brilliant,
and universal peace of earth, and not a particle of their flesh or a hair of their heads or
bodies injured: they would still exist and
move by the force of their will, and by the
spirit of life that God gave them.   The animal
power of the earth is thus subjected to the
divine power of man and the animals, which
emanates from heaven; the carnal is subjected to the spiritual.   The wicked are cut off in
their ways because desire has failed and want
fled, and the world is thus triumphantly, for
the time, redeemed and metamorphosed into
a paradise or heaven.

There is no longer any necessity for labor,

occupations are cut short, and the world would be inquiring for truth instead of error and wrong; hence, what a magnificent opportunity for a preacher to preach the Gospel! All are ready and anxious to listen—the way is fully prepared—the throne of heaven is addressed—Christ and the saints of earth and heaven can suffer no violence here. So the opportunity is now propitious, the decree of heaven forbidding their visit is suspended during this peace, and they may be seen coming, as it were, in clouds of light from heaven, not in the frailty of the flesh, but in power and glory.

St. John, in the 20th chapter of Revelations, gives a description of the millennium and the reign of Christ and his saints on earth for a thousand years; but the better hypothesis is that their reign will be co-extensive with the peace of earth, and not a moment longer, let that be a thousand years or a day, as the case may be. Christ also, in the 24th chapter of Matthew, gives a very clear statement of his second advent on earth; and from this statement as well as from reason we may conclude

19

very properly that his second advent on earth
is because of and the result of peace, and his
coming not the cause of peace. In other words,
the serene peace of earth will prepare the way
of Christ and his angels to visit this earth;—
this will be the first resurrection according to
St. John, that is, the first appearance of the
redeemed of earth to its portals. They do not
rise from the grave, but descend in clouds
with him from heaven. "Death hath no more
dominion over them."

Now, if we can, it behooves us to search and
ascertain what power, if any, can bring about
this peace and secure these results. We cannot for a moment believe that God governs the
heavens and the earth by caprice or personal
attention, but by laws positive and certain;
and the power to establish this peace must be
immense, and not any idle or capricious power
exerted at leisure or random. It is more probable that it was ordained from the beginning,
and must occur in the regular order of nature.
Consequently, we must consult the movements
of the heavenly bodies to learn and ascertain

this power; for we all well know that there is no power on earth that can accomplish it.

There is the best of reasons for asserting that the millennium will occur by the passage of a heavenly body—such as a star, sun, or comet, if you choose—in the regular course of its orbit, assigned it from the beginning of time, so near our earth as to overcome or counteract, for the time, the influence of the sun, moon and stars, and produce the results we have just described; that is, it will banish heat, cold, hunger, thirst, pain, desire, decay, and death. It must have, by its size or proximity to our earth, an overwhelming power—nullifying, during its passage, the attraction of the sun, moon and stars, and, for the time being, shed the most transcendent light over the whole earth. The fire maniacs of the world will, no doubt, tremble with fear on the approach of such a sublime visiter, and will expect to be burned up and the earth melted with fervent heat. No such thing can transpire, for heaven is not composed of fire, but of light, life, peace, good-will: and architecture, as planets, suns, moons, &c.   Light, as before shown in chapter on Earth, possesses no heat; neither do the rays of the sun; if so, they would melt the snow and ice from the ice-capped mountains in the tropics.   And the simple fact that such snow-capped mountains exist nearly under the equator teaches mankind that neither the sun nor its rays possess heat, and that the cause of heat must be looked for from other sources than heaven.   Light, as before stated, is a powerful element of heaven, and life is the same, and both emanate from the omnipotence of heaven.

In our own time we have seen one of these visitors—though, perhaps, not large and powerful enough to accomplish such mighty results as just described—traversing the heavens above us.   This was the comet of 1858.   No doubt it was performing its revolution around its proper centre in the course of nature assigned it, and at a certain fixed time it will return and traverse the identical space that it did in the summer of 1858.   It must not be assumed that its passage was by chance, or left to uncertainty: but the correct theory is that it was performing the mission of its Creator, and will do so through all eternity. Having no will or choice of its own, it can only obey that of its Creator. It may require that comet centuries or thousands of years to return, but it will as certainly return as time and the heavens endure. Other comets, more magnificent than that, have appeared; smaller comets also frequently appear; some are quite small, and are very distant. Some, it is said, approach very near to the sun; so, if they were vapors, or nebulous matter, they would be consumed by the heat of the sun if the sun possessed heat, as some suppose. Their orbits are eccentric, which proves the theory, heretofore advanced, that there are repulsive forces governing the heavenly bodies, and therefore no collisions can occur among them.

My views of the millenium, if chimerical, are derived from the Bible; and, when we consider the immutability of the laws of nature, and also the scriptural evidences, they must have at least some claims to credence.

We will now briefly examine the scriptural evidences of the cause, nature, and results of the millennium. We will first examine the 24th chapter of Matthew, which contains a description of it, and make some remarks as to the time of its occurrence; after which, we will examine St. John's description contained in several chapters of Revelations.

"And as he sat upon the mount of Olives, the disciples came unto him privately, saying, Tell us, when shall these things be? And what shall be the sign of thy coming, and of the end of the world?" (v. 3.) Christ, it must here be remembered, had informed his disciples that he was to be crucified, and would leave them a little while. "And Jesus answered and said unto them, Take heed that no man deceive you. For many shall come in my name, saying, I am Christ; and shall deceive many." He then informed them that they should hear of wars and rumors of wars; that kingdoms and nations would rise against each other; that there would be famines and earthquakes and also pestilences in divers places · "but the end is not yet." He also said that false prophets should arise, and that this Gospel of the kingdom should be preached in all the world for a witness unto all nations.

Now, from his remarks we would very naturally infer that a great lapse of time must occur from his crucifixion and departure till his return or second advent to earth. The preceding remarks have reference as to the time, from which it will be seen that no man can tell or know precisely. Now we will proceed and examine his description of it.

"When ye, therefore, shall see the abomination of desolation, spoken of by Daniel the prophet, stand in the holy place (whoso readeth, let him understand)"—this probably has reference to the 7th chapter of Daniel, and the "casting down of thrones," and the sitting or reign of the "Ancient of days" or Christ himself; and probably also the 12th chapter, and the "trouble," and resurrection of the saints unto "everlasting life, and some to shame and everlasting contempt." Christ says, "For then shall be great tribulation, such as was not since the beginning of the world to this time, no, nor ever shall be. And except those days should be shortened, there should no flesh be saved: but for the elect's sake those days shall be shortened." This language proves conclusively that his description is not of the end of the world, but of his second advent; for time and the world are to move on again for the elect's sake.

It might be asked, in this connection, who the elect are for whom those days are shortened, whether they are of earth or heaven, and what is meant by the flesh being saved. The rational view of these matters is this:—The elect to be thus favored are the saints of God who dwell in heaven. Transgression occurs in heaven; earth is the place of atonement, and the flesh is the manner of regeneration and redemption of transgressors. If the flesh of the earth is cut off, the elect will suffer for means wherewith to punish transgressors. This view may seem far-fetched to the reader, but the condition of this earth is only to be reconciled with the omnipotence and goodness of God by ascribing to it a penal and regenerating nature. Revelation says that the dragon and his angels were cast out from heaven to earth, and that Adam was driven out of Eden to till the ground. St. Peter said, "For if God spared not the angels of heaven that sinned, but cast them down to hell, and delivered them into chains of darkness to be reserved unto judgment," &c. (See 2 Pet. ii. and Rev. xii.) From these, it appears that the elect to be favored by saving the flesh of earth are those of heaven, as the elect of earth might be saved (as those of heaven were) through obedience and regeneration unto everlasting life.

Christ then again admonishes the people of false prophets who shall show great signs and wonders, so as to deceive, if it were possible, even the elect. He says, "I have told you before" (that is, of false prophets). "Wherefore, if they shall say unto you, Behold, he is in the desert; go not forth: Behold, he is in the secret chambers; believe it not. For as the lightning cometh out of the east, and shineth even unto the west, so shall also the coming of the son of man be. For wheresoever the carcass is, there will the eagles be gathered together. Immediately after the tribulation of those days shall the sun be darkened, and the moon shall not give her ligh , and the stars shall fall from heaven, and the powers of the heavens shall be shaken." Now here we have a description of the events that must first occur before he makes his second advent; for, mark you, he has not re-appeared yet; but the way is now prepared ready for him and his angels. The carcass is ready, for desire, pain, sin, and death, are abolished or suspended by these mighty forerunners of their coming.

In the next verse he says, "And then shall appear the sign of the Son of man in heaven: and then shall all the tribes of the earth mourn, and they shall see the Son of man coming in the clouds of heaven, with power and great glory." Again he says, "Now learn a parable of the fig-tree: when his branch is yet tender, and putteth forth leaves, ye know that summer is nigh : so likewise when ye shall see all these things. know that it is near, even at the doors." He then proceeds to affirm that "this generation shall not pass till all these things be fulfilled"; that heaven and earth should pass away, but his words should not. The word "generation," as used by him, was used in its general sense, and includes the races of men and animals, &c., of earth, and not a particular set of them.

From this description, it is self-evident to all that Christ will not visit this earth till the way is prepared. This preparation is likened to a carcass, and Christ's and his saints' coming to that of eagles. What power, then, must the people of this earth look to as the proper one to prepare the way? From Christ's description, and that of St. John in Revelation, which will be noticed presently, it must be a heavenly body more luminous than the sun, either from its size or proximity to the earth. God is not a being of projects and whims, but a firm and consistent Governor of the heavens. He does not govern to please the fancy of the degraded of earth, or excite their curiosity or fear, but to edify, instruct, and entertain. So

when the earth is blessed with the millennium
and the republication of truth, it will be by
the exercise of His laws and goodness as ordained from the foundation of the world.

St. John speaks of the four winds being
holden by four angels standing on the four
corners of the earth, so that they blew not on
the earth. Again John says, "I saw a star
fall from heaven unto the earth : and to him
was given the key of the bottomless pit. And
he opened the bottomless pit," &c. Here we
have a positive scriptural assertion that the
bottomless pit is to be opened by reason of the
falling of a star from heaven to earth. By the
falling or approach of this star, or celestial
body, a light so luminous and resplendent
may envelope and overspread the earth as to
darken the sun, the moon may not give her
light, and the stars so completely overshad-
owed that it may be said they have fallen from
heaven. What other power can the people of
earth look for to shake the powers of the heavens as described by Christ? It must be a powerful celestial body possessing the exceeding

brilliancy requisite to obscure the sun, moon, and stars; and by its progress or flight through the heavens, in its orbit, their powers will be shaken; not by violence, but its visit and presence among them will be graciously recognized and approved by a bow in the nature of obeisance and welcome. No collision can take place, for smaller celestial bodies may bow themselves out of its way, if necessary, by the aid of the light of heaven; or it may bow itself out of their way, as is proved by the eccentric courses of these visitors.

These things must occur, and they will occur gradually, before Christ makes his advent. They occur gradually, which he likens to the putting forth leaves on the tender branches of the fig-tree. The appearance of a celestial body would have a like resemblance. We may look for it in the east; and it will be as plain as lightning in the east, and shine even to the west; that is, it will not be partial in its nature, but envelope the whole earth with light as brilliant as lightning itself. On its first appearance, it will envelope the earth with its refulgent light by degrees, just as the heats of spring cover the fig-tree with foliage. So pseudo-prophets need not and must not ever be consulted, or even listened to: the fact will be patent and powerfully visible to all. Now this is what must be done before Christ appears with his saints, which will be in power and clouds of glory.

Now let us examine the effects of this occurrence. He says, "When ye shall see the abomination of desolation, spoken of by Daniel the prophet," &c., that the kings of the earth will tremble, and thrones will be cast down, and the people of the earth will mourn because of great tribulation, and the Ancient of days will sit — that is, truth reign omnipotent—for error is cast down and fled from the earth. The truth, the omnipotent truth, is emblazoned in the heavens, and error is discarded. Christ says, "Let them which be in Judea flee into the mountains"—that means getting suitable situations to enjoy and observe the millennium, for the strife of earth is to be banished, and with it pain, desire, sin, and death :

"Let him which is on the house-top not come down to take anything out of his house"— for hunger and thirst have fled, and he will have no need of food or drink: "Neither let him which is in the field return back to take his clothes"—because heat, cold, wet, &c., are all driven away, and he will have no need of them. And he even goes so far as to allude to females in a delicate situation, and those that give suck. All strife, pain, and generation being suspended, of course parturition or births cannot occur; hence their state during the millennium. These instances teach that profound peace must be caused on earth during the millennium. The wind will not even blow, a leaf will not be moved, nor a single cloud, nor mist or dust be seen; but the whole heavens and earth must be enveloped with light, power, glory, and truth. Then look for the sign of Christ and his saints coming in power and great glory; not a few angels with him, but clouds of them, as brilliant as the sun. Then the people of earth will see and hear the truth of the Gospel for themselves, and see whether it consists of metaphysical creeds and empty ceremonies, or whether religion is a plain duty that all owe to God and their neighbor, let that neighbor be who or what creature it may.

The description of the millennium so completely resembles that of a celestial body in its orbit, first approaching our earth and then encompassing it with its light, &c., that it is quite reasonable to suppose it will occur and pass by just in that manner. We will examine other scriptural authorities to corroborate this view. In the 7th chapter of Revelations, St. John says, "And after these things [speaking of the opening of the seals] I saw four angels standing on the four corners of the earth, holding the four winds of the earth, that the wind should not blow on the earth, nor on the sea, nor on any tree." Now here is a state of the utmost peace described; and in the preceding chapter he said, "The sun became as black as sackcloth of hair, and the moon became as blood, and the stars of heaven fell unto the earth." Then he mentions the four angels holding the four winds, and then says, "And I saw another angel ascending from the east, having the seal of the living God." This is, without controversy, Christ and his second advent, for the description here and in Matthew correspond too closely to admit of doubt.

In the 9th chapter of Revelations, St. John says, "And the fifth angel sounded, and I saw a star fall from heaven unto earth, and to him was given the key of the bottomless pit. And he opened the bottomless pit; and there arose a smoke out of the pit, as the smoke of a great furnace; and the sun and the air were darkened by reason of the smoke of the pit." The word "star" occurs in this description, which has direct allusion to the millennium. Here a star is represented as falling to earth, which may mean the passage of the star in its orbit. It had the key of the bottomless pit; that is, power over the flesh and strife of the earth. It could, by the action of its light, banish the wants, pain, desire, strife, and death from the earth, and thus bind Satan. The smoke represents sin, &c., &c., as disappearing; and the

20

darkening of the sun may be attributed to its resplendent light.

The remainder of the chapter probably has reference to events that shall occur after the millennium. St. John then speaks of "mighty angels," which clearly proves that there are grades of beings in heaven as well as earth.

In the 20th chapter of Revelations, St. John again takes up this subject and speaks as follows: "And I saw an angel come down from heaven, having the key of the bottomless pit and a great chain in his hand. And he laid hold on the dragon, that old serpent which is the Devil, and Satan, and bound him a thousand years, and cast him into the bottomless pit, and shut him up, and set a seal upon him, that he should deceive the nations no more, till the thousand years should be fulfilled: and after that he must be loosed a little season." The "key of the bottomless pit" here mentioned signifies power over the flesh and sin of this world; the chain also represents power; the laying hold and binding the dragon signifies the subduing the powers of this earth; and the casting into the bottomless pit represents the banishment of sin, desire, want, hunger, thirst, pain, death, &c. This is the preparation for Christ's advent. Then St. John goes on to speak of the thrones and souls of martyrs. and those that had not worshipped the beast—meaning the flesh of earth, or self-worship—and that they lived and reigned with Christ a thousand years. " But the rest of the dead," he says, "lived not again till the thousand years were finished. This is the first resurrection"—that is, the first appearance of our departed friends on earth since their carnal death. They come not from the grave, but, as Christ told the apostles, with him from heaven, in power and great glory. This idea that some people entertain, that the souls of men slumber in the grave for a specific judgment-day, is preposterous. and the text here proves it so; and so does Christ's remark to the thief on the cross, for he was to go and be in paradise with him that day, and not to the grave. The day of judgment is general, and includes all time, and is the day of death to each one.

St. John says, "the rest of the dead lived not again till the thousand years were finished." The question here presents itself, who are "the rest of the dead that lived not again?" They evidently mean the inhabitants of this earth who shall witness the millennial reign. They are spiritually dead, and must suffer carnal death and be regenerated before they can enjoy the life and glory of the saints. As strife, the mystery of earth, is overcome by the millennium, death cannot ensue; so they must wait for their death and regeneration till the thousand years here spoken of be finished. He says, "Blessed and holy is he that hath part in the first resurrection: on such the second death hath no power, but they shall be priests of God and of Christ, and shall reign with him a thousand years."

After this Satan is to be loosed out of his prison, "and shall go out to deceive the nations which are in the four quarters of the earth, Gog and Magog, to gather them together to battle: the number of whom is as the sand of the sea." Here we have positive assurance that the millennium is not perpetual, but of a transitory nature, such as would be produced by the passage of a heavenly body in its orbit. As to the length of time that this reign will occupy, it is not by any means probable that it will be a thousand years. A thousand years and a day are equivalent terms in prophetic language. The better opinion would seem to be that it would not last sufficiently long to injure the people or the vegetation of earth; for what would injure vegetation would injure the inhabitants of earth. God has the creatures of earth in process of regeneration, and intends to instruct and regenerate the whole of them in due time, and would not be likely to do any act that would frustrate His own designs.

We have now taken a view of the approach and continuance of the millennium, and will proceed to consider the end and results of it. If the theory advanced is correct, the millennium will pass by in like gradual manner as it came; the celestial visitor will speed by on its way through its orbit, and as it leaves our

horizon its influence will be gradually relaxed; the illumination caused by its approach
and proximity will grow less resplendent. till
at length it will have attained such a great
distance from the earth and our solar system
that its power and influence will be no longer
overwhelming. The rays of the sun will then
penetrate our atmosphere and again set the
strife of the earth in motion; the moon will
then give her light, and the stars seem to re-
gain their places; and as the visitor speeds
clear away, the world will wake up to a vivid
sense of their desolate and forlorn condition.
The Devil or Satan will again be loosed on
earth, and desire, pain, hunger thirst, disease,
and death, again triumphantly reign. Mankind again see the necessity of labor to sup-
ply their wants, hence they proceed to their
accustomed occupations, and the world moves
on as usual. But they now have the light of
divine truth, for God's will has been manifested, and His promises to mankind have been
renewed. The resurrection of the dead to an
eternal heaven, and to the enjoyment of re-

wards according to their works, have been powerfully manifested to both small and great. This manifestation has been so brilliant that all rational and irrational creatures of earth have witnessed it. So grand has the illumination been, that even the insects of the soil and the corals of the sea became affected by it, and were made witnesses of the event.

Mankind will largely profit by this event, and will multiply and become very numerous on earth in the course of time. The first few generations will be true believers in this millennium and will be strict observers of truth; but as time progresses succeeding generations will become skeptical, and finally in the great lapse of time the event will be discredited, and mankind will regard it as a fable or fabrication of religious zealots, or a pagan superstition. Science will advance by means of this celestial visitation, and it is to be hoped that discoveries will be made whereby man may greatly improve his condition both on earth and in eternity.

Similar events have, without the least doubt,

heretofore occurred, and by such means the ancients derived their knowledge of the resurrection of the dead, and also of heaven. The fallen and forlorn condition of the world is apparent without the aid of revelation, but the manner of this fall, the cause and the manner of the creation of the world has been revealed by former millenniums. These periods, because of the barrenness of language and the backward state of science, are quite imperfectly recorded by the ancients; but still enough is recorded to satisfy any reasonable mind that will investigate the subject, that millennial reigns have formerly occurred. How much more reasonable and satisfactory is this opinion of revelation than the partial modes described by Moses!

Moses gives a narrative of an interview with God on Mt. Sinai in the 19th chapter of Exodus, but his account is merely a figurative description of some former event, and is, withal, blended with some of the superstitions of that age; but in his description we have the main features of the millennium. He says, "Mount

Sinai was altogether on a smoke, because the Lord descended upon it in fire." This fire can only represent a former millennial illumination, for it is highly improbable that God would choose such a destructive and vicious element in which to make His appearance on earth; and besides, He is not so partial as to give a few people of earth such blessings to the exclusion of others. God, in His visitations, is just to all, even to the worms of the dust. Moses could not have gone upon the mount if it was on fire, as some people imagine. The truth of this matter is, Moses had an account, though very imperfect, of a former millennium, and in the barrenness of the language at his command he gave us the best narrative of it he could. He went so far as to teach that God was a "consuming fire"; not that he, or any one else, had ever seen Him— for Christ teaches differently—but because he had received quite authentic accounts from the antediluvians who witnessed and handed down by tradition accounts of such millennial reigns. We are not, however, to censure or to blame Moses for his imperfect descriptions, or his figures of speech, nor even for interpolating some of the superstitions of that time; because he was himself a man, and therefore not perfect; neither was his language or his memory. Without doubt he did the best he could to enlighten mankind. His laws were mostly just, and should even be obeyed at this day as divine truths, except those that were pointedly condemned by Christ, and are also to be condemned by reason. Such were never received from God, but are the work of men. God's word and truth is sanctioned by justice and reason; and whatever conflicts with these, either in the Bible or elsewhere, is of earth, and not to be believed or practised.

Moses was inclined to, and did give mankind the best record in his power of the knowledge the antediluvians possessed concerning God and His works and laws. Christ gave his apostles as plain a description of his second advent as he could without incurring the risk of being called a liar and impostor. If in that day he had told the apostles and the world that the way would be prepared for his second advent by a comet, or heavenly body, as large perhaps as a million of such earths as this, and more luminous than the sun, he would have been disbelieved. He likened the kingdom of God to a grain of mustard-seed, which when planted grew and waxed a great tree, so large that the fowls of the air lodged in its branches. This decisively proves, if proof was needed, that heaven embraces the whole starry creation. It also proves that the heavens are productive powers, and are gaining in volume and power. Hence I have before affirmed that the light of heaven exerts a productive influence, and that matter or material spheres, as planets, &c., are increasing and growing larger.

Christ also likened the kingdom of God to leaven hid in meal till the whole was leavened. (See these similitudes as recorded in the 13th chapter of St. Luke's Gospel.) Now if he had told his disciples and apostles that the light emanating from the luminaries of heaven was this leaven, and that it was powerful enough to drive off at a proper distance from them and float worlds like this; and not only this, but to drive them in their orbits around them and around each other, and to cause them to revolve on their own axes, causing day and night, he would have been reckoned a maniac or an impostor. So he contented himself by explaining this matter just as he did, well knowing that his meaning would be unfolded by science and investigation. The leaven in the meal is clearly typical of the light of heaven, which raises and sustains the heavens and spreads them out before our eyes: and if any further proof were needed of Christ's divinity, mankind have it in the truth of my discovery and philosophy. Science will now prove his divinity, and all skepticism and doubt as to the resurrection of the dead, as taught by him, forever banished.

If I am correct in affirming that the millennium will occur by the passage of some celestial body in its orbit, it must come, as comets do, from another solar system than our own, or any in our horizon even. I assert that our solar system is an inferior one, and that another and another system crowns it; and that all these systems are composed of light and substances of their own peculiar kind. They yield and bring forth after their kind just as pictured in the objects here of earth. I assert also that there is one grand system— or third heaven, if you please, spoken of by St. Paul—that crowns the whole. The light of each of these systems or suns is different, but of the precise quality required to sustain and drive the planets of that system; and so of all the suns or solar systems of the Universe. The light of one would not probably drive the planets of another. Hence we see comets or celestial bodies passing through our own and through other systems. They seem to be independent, in some measure, of any system known to us, and are so; and are doubtless driven by suns, situated in the far-distant heavens, which are and must forever remain unknown to mankind. By one of these distant suns, the celestial body that is to prepare the way of the millennium must be driven in its orbit. Near the centre of this system, without doubt, is the abode of God, and perhaps of Christ and his elect.

This event, though an astronomical one, may be distant;—it may be at our doors. "But of that day and hour knoweth no man, no, not the angels of heaven, but my Father only"—so says Christ in his description of it; and this should silence false prophets forever, for, without controversy, the event will be an astronomical one, and is not the subject of prophecy. "Watch therefore; for ye know not at what hour your Lord doth come."

THE END.